Table of Contents

INTRODUCTION

Get Hired- Job Interview Success Tips, Skills, and Strategies

Ace your job interviews and get hired for the jobs you want.

Master the art of selling your knowledge and talent to hiring managers using the job interview tips, skills, and strategies found in this book to stand out from the competition and land your dream job.

Talking about yourself is tricky business. Some of us are uncomfortable doing it. Others engage too freely. Striking the right balance in your personal and professional life is an art. But nowhere is it more important than in a job interview.

After weeks of preparation and tirelessly searching for positions that fit your credentials, you're granted an interview. That single meeting can make or break your chances of getting hired. You may have the right skills and be a perfect fit for the job, but if you don't know how to sell yourself properly, you'll quickly be out of the running and back to square one.

Even the most prepared of us get nervous. And sometimes, fear takes over— negatively affecting performance. Perhaps, you're regularly granted interviews and subsequently rejected for job after job. You wonder what you've missed and obsess over questions you could have answered differently or things you should have mentioned. The more you interview without result, the more disheartened you become. The experience begins to wear down your confidence— sabotaging future interviews. It's a difficult cycle to break, but it can be done.

Interview Tips: Proven Job Interview Tips, Interview Questions and Interview Skills to Get Hired in Job Interviews for the Job You Want was written to help you get to the bottom of what's not working and start doing what will work in your job interviews and get hired.

Before making any adjustments to your interview style, you will learn how to figure out the reasons why you are not being hired. Only once you determine what's holding you back, can you begin perfecting the art of:

- Successfully selling yourself in a job interview

- Turning job interviews into job offers

- Negotiating your best salary

In the end, it all comes down to effective interview skills and a winning getting hired job interview strategy. Having the right job interview strategy will increase your confidence and give you a 50% greater chance of being hired. There is no cookie-cutter strategy. Your strategy must be crafted to highlight your best qualities and make you more memorable and stand out from the other job candidates interviewing for the same position. **Interview Tips: Proven Job Interview Tips, Interview Questions, and Interview Skills to Get Hired in Job Interviews for the Job You Want** gives you the information to develop a strategy that will increase your chances of landing your dream job.

Effective communication skills are imperative in all aspects of life. And when it comes to job interviews, you need to be on top of your communication game. In a short period, you are tasked with demonstrating to someone you've never met that you are the perfect candidate for a job. Your words, appearance, nonverbal cues and more will be judged and deemed adequate or not.

Interview Tips: Proven Job Interview Tips, Interview Questions, and Interview Skills to Get Hired in Job Interviews for the Job You Want offers advise on knowing what to say and how to act, including specific things most interviewers want to hear. You'll build your confidence and learn how to sell yourself in a way that will make people want you for their organization.

Your dream job is waiting and it's time you took the steps necessary to land it.

Interview Tips: Proven Job Interview Tips, Interview Questions and Interview Skills to Get Hired in Job Interviews for the Job You Want is dedicated to helping anyone out there who wants a competitive edge interviewing for jobs:

- ❖ Increase confidence— even when you've faced past rejection.

- ❖ Articulate your story— striking the perfect balance.

- ❖ Highlight your knowledge and skill-set for the position at hand.

- ❖ Tackle tough interview questions with ease.

- ❖ Identify questions you should ask during an interview and ones to avoid.

- ❖ Negotiate your best salary.

- ❖ Close your interview by "Asking for the Job."

- ❖ Follow-up the correct way.

- ❖ Stand out in a way that makes you an irresistible hire.

When it comes to interview, there is no such thing as being over-prepared. Once you master these techniques, you will stand apart from other job candidates and get the results you're looking for. Success begets success and the edge you gain will show in everything you do— from landing your dream job to performing its essential duties once you're hired.

Start learning today the job interview tips, skills, and strategies you need to know to get hired.

The only thing standing between you and getting hired for the job you want is having the right job interview tips, skills, and strategies to have a successful job interview.

Gaining your job interview edge today.

Get Hired for the Job You Want!

CHAPTER 1

GET HIRED – BUILDING THE CONFIDENT YOU

A confident persona appeals more to everyone than a nervous one. Self-confidence is one quality that is crucial for you to have as an interviewee and can make a world of difference for you. As a confident person, you exhibit a personality that states your openness and willingness to work, your belief in your abilities and knowledge and your level of optimism and positivity amidst a stressful situation. It shows your ability to persuade others and as such may convince the interviewer to give you the job, keeping the other requirements in consideration of course. Given the situation, it is alright to feel a little nervous before the interview as this shows how much this job means to you. But if it makes you fumble or too paralyzed to express yourself during the interview, then you may be over-thinking the whole thing. You need not to only gain the confidence of the interviewer but be able to inspire them too, and your own show of confidence will give you the upper hand in landing your dream job. Remember, confidence does not just stem from knowing everything but also from knowing the right things, answering the right things and admitting the right things.

Given below are tips to build and boost your confidence for facing the interview:

10 WAYS TO BUILD AND INCREASE YOUR JOB INTERVIEW CONFIDENCE

Follow these steps to work towards boosting your confidence and with constant practice, see yourself transform into a confident and relaxed you. It is always better to be well-prepared than to be overwhelmed by the interviewing process.

Research the company

To begin with, you must know who you are applying for and what are their goals, objectives, policies, and beliefs. This information will help you identify their expectations for the post they offer, your expected role in the company and how you can address it or make it better. You can find this information, along with the information for company's employees, on the company's own website. Review the jobs that interest you, so that you can play it to your strengths. Expand your research by exploring the portals for company reviews, or by visiting corporate investigation bureaus, etc., to find any registered complaints or shortcomings in the company's environment and how it can potentially affect or empower your role. It is essential to know that your professional goals and beliefs align with those of your employers to ensure job satisfaction and security. This preliminary research will help you to gain insight about the company and its values and give you an advantage during the interview.

Prepare your responses

Make a note of the several commonly asked questions during the interview: ranging from the knowledge of the domain to the knowledge of yourself. Research the top questions asked by the companies in your domain: what are they most likely to ask of you? These will certainly vary if you are an inexperienced or an experienced person. How will you tell them about yourself? Make a print out of these questions and pose your answers to them in a notebook. Evaluate your own replies till you are satisfied; choose words that best highlight your talents and skills in your domain, words that are true to your qualification and present you as a professional. You don't want to sit in an interview and informally blabber about yourself with complete frankness or offer formal, repetitive replies and sound insincere. You have to keep it honest and to the point. Think of these 4 C's- clear , concise , convincing and compelling.

Practice and Rehearse

Now that you have crafted your best responses and are satisfied with it, you must be able to articulate them without sounding fake or by reading your note cards. This can only be possible if you practice your responses until it feels natural. You need to sound like you just came up with the response. Do not rush through the answer and take appropriate breaths as you relay it. Practice before a mirror so you can evaluate yourself or have a friend work with you. You can make use of response cards initially in your practice to aid you as you trip or stutter, but memorize your responses so you can rid yourself of the cards soon. In case you have trouble recalling the exact structure of your response, then try memorizing the key highlights within it so you can frame your response around those. Keep practicing to make sure you have the core of your answers memorized so much that it comes naturally to you without any stammering or filler words that indicate you are crafting your responses then and there. Focus on the clarity and pitch of your voice as well as your tone of speaking too while you practice your responses.

Watch your body language

Your verbal responses are not the only thing the interviewer will take note of. Your body language and postures speak with a volume of their own. Along with the practice of the verbal responses, take note of your body postures and gestures and evaluate them critically or have someone else point out the flaws for you through a mock interview. Do you sit straight or have a habit of slouching or slumping with time? Do you appear friendly in general or do you come off as defensive? How often do you make use of your hands and in what manner? Is it just to emphasize your point or to buy time while you work up a response? Make sure you are seated upright with your head high and your hands in your lap and feet even with the floor. Have an optimistic smile on your face and keep a decent eye contact with the interviewer. Practice on a good and decent nonverbal communication.

Image is Everything

Dress to impress for the job interview. Transform yourself with the right ensemble for the event: one that portrays your best self while remaining within the company's dress code. This shows your willingness and ability to fit into the company's environment. Choose colors that are neither too bright nor too flashy as they could pose a distraction for the interviewer. Find something that makes you feel comfortable, stylish and confident but still brings out the professional side of you. Always remember it is best to overdress for a job interview than to be underdressed. Make your best first impression by dressing for success.

Handle your skeletons

Companies do a background check on their would-be employees, so it's better to keep a check on yourself to avoid any surprise questioning. Be honest about your own career history. Research yourself online to make sure you have no presentation that could be negatively interpreted and used against you as a result of your social media interactions. Anything you post or share on your social media can be interpreted as defining you and your personality. Handle these skeletons appropriately by preparing responses for them rather than brushing it aside and hoping they are not discovered.

List insightful Questions

As an interviewee, it is profiting to prepare your own set of questions to ask during an interview as this reflects on your interest in working for the company, as well as your knowledge on the expected role and the intended domain of work. Carefully craft your questions and avoid asking about the information that is easily researched and available on the company's website.

Think confident to stay confident

The simplest way to stay confident is by thinking confidently about yourself, but this is certainly the hardest part to achieve if you are overcritical of yourself. Remind yourself of the positive things about you, remember that you have the potential and knowledge for this job and that is just why your résumé got selected. Motivate yourself with positive assertions to stay confident and repeat them until it becomes genuine.

Pep talk with friends

Get your friends and family to give you a pep talk and boost your confidence in yourself. Have them tell you about your innate qualities and abilities, your skills as a communicator and a team player.

Make the Decision

You must be decisive about what you want or don't want. Are you willing to do everything to get this job? Do you feel secure with the information you have gathered about the company? Does the salary compensate your work requirements and needs? Making a firm decision regarding your job can help in providing the final boost to your confidence. Question yourself on these aspects; think about what you are giving way to achieve what you want and how the presence of this job affects you and your situation. Do not shy away from questioning and answering yourself as ultimately any of these can be the factors that motivate you. Now that you are satisfied with your position, you can creatively contribute to the company's growth too.

10 JOB INTERVIEW SUCCESS STRATEGIES FOR A CONFIDENT YOU

As the day of your interview nears, don't let your stress overwhelm you. Instead, prepare your mind for presenting the best and professional version of yourself and picture yourself confidently going through the interview. Keep up with your preparation as it is never enough and when the time comes, give it all you have got to offer.

On the day of the interview, equip yourself with these proven strategies to ensure you successfully achieve your goal with a favorable conclusion, all the while building your confidence:

Be prepared for the interview

Proper preparation before an interview is essential to ensure your success in an interview as well as to give you a well of confidence for facing the interview. Do the research about the company that has called you and about the job role you have applied for. Prepare the possible questions that you will be asked and the questions that you need to ask. Practice your verbal responses and your nonverbal communication till you get it to come naturally to you. Work on your personal presentation; dress as it seems fit for the interview– with a touch of yourself to give you comfort– and neatly arrange all your documents in a portfolio, accessible by relevance. Stay punctual and show up on time for the interview. If you are unaware of the venue, then take time, a day before the interview, for a preliminary inspection of the location. All this preparation and hard work you do will add up to your success in getting the job.

Stay calm

Before you are called for the interview, stay calm and collected. Wait patiently for your turn to be called and if you feel restless, occupy yourself with something constructive like reading the company brochure and taking notes or preparing further questions for asking during the interview. Even during the interview, maintain a calm personality. Sit in a comfortable position without appearing informal or unprofessional and take slow breaths to even yourself. Politely address the interviewer and keep your focus on them and what they say to dispel your own thoughts. Keep your tone level and your voice clear enough to be heard.

Use positive nonverbal communication

You need to maintain professionalism with your gestures as it eventually adds up to understanding "who you are" as a person. So, use your nonverbal communication to your advantage. During the interview, sit comfortably yet attentively and keep your hands on your lap when you are not using them for any demonstrations. Do not constantly shift your body as this displays your restlessness. Do not make an excessive use of your hands or any other action that causes a distraction to the interviewer or signals a wrong impression of you. Do not cross your legs, one over the other but keep them flat on the ground. Maintain a decent eye contact with the interviewer and gently smile as these convey your determination and optimism during the interview.

Professionally connect with your interviewer

You need to maintain a polite and decent connection with the interviewer in order to gain their confidence as well as boost your own. Shake hands with them and greet them a good day as you walk in for the interview and keep smiling throughout the interview session. Speak levelly and make use of professional jargon rather than slangs. Maintain the same level of professional cordiality as you present your own questions to them. You can also take the liberty to ask questions about themselves, their job and the work environment, with respect to their position. Establishing this connection with your interviewer can increase your chances of being hired. Don't forget to thank them for their time and bid them a good day as you leave the interview room.

Stay true

To maintain your confidence and comfort during the interview, it is important to stay true to yourself and as such stay honest with the interviewer. And while you need to stay true to yourself, you need to remember to be professional so that you are projecting the image of who you are professionally and how appropriate you are for the job.

Listen keenly

Listen to your interviewer and clearly understand what they are saying; they may be inquiring about you or detailing you about the company and its requirements. Any information that they relay to you is important as it could be used to tailor your own responses or inquiries. More importantly, it shows that you have been listening and paying attention to them, and are capable of attentively answering to the needs of your employers, co-workers and customers. Listening carefully to your interviewers also aids you in maintaining clarity and dispelling any fears.

Answer only what is asked

As stated earlier, understanding what is being asked of you is essential in order to respond appropriately. If you are unsure of the query, then politely ask for further clarification instead of providing an answer that does not tally with the inquiry. This ambiguity can happen when the interviewer poses a question that is somehow related to your knowledge or to your prepared set of questions and answers. Tweak your responses to the questions as they are asked.

Give Examples

Instead of offering vague responses, it is beneficial to furnish your answers with concrete examples of how you have employed your skills previously to achieve customer satisfaction. Set these examples to highlight your talents as a skilled communicator and a problem solver. This not only portrays your successful performance in the past but it is also an indicator of your expected performance in the future. Give the Interviewer/ Hiring Manager an example of a work-related problem you solved. Clearly state the **problem**, **solution** and **result** using the Problem Solution Result method also known as the PSR (P=Problem,S=Solution, R=Result) method. Use the following formula to explain your problem-solving skills in job interviews. The Problem Solution Result (PSR) method will help set you apart from your competition and impress the hiring managing on your problem-solving skills.

Ask questions

Research the companies business objectives, needs, challenges, competitors, products, and services thoroughly and prepare a set of questions before the interview as it shows your preparation for the interview. Get a clear understanding of the company's mission statement and the vision the CEO has for the company. During the interview, expand the list of questions that you may have by listening to what the interviewer has to say. Try to gain further information regarding the company from the interviewer.

Stay optimistic

Post interview, follow up with a thank-you email or mail a note to the interviewer a day later and drop all your worries about the outcome. Continue with your learning and practice to further build your character and confidence. In the thank-you note, continue to sell the value that you will bring to the company. Try to list 3 clear and concise bullet points. Remember you are always "selling" your knowledge, talents and skills, even in a thank-you note. And tell the interviewer how excited you are about the job opportunity.

Using these tested strategies and tips, prepare yourself and gain confidence to get the job you want.

CHAPTER 2

HOW TO THOUGHTFULLY CRAFT YOUR "TELL ME ABOUT YOURSELF" RESPONSE

One of the obvious and yet the most dreaded question in any interview is *"Tell me about yourself."*

It is only a general question, one that you can certainly answer. Yet somehow, this question can either cause you to struggle to come up with an elaborate response or blunder as you come up with irrelevant responses.

As open-ended as this question is, in an interview, you cannot come up with any response that comes to your mind; everything you say must be clearly planned in your mind with the goal to highlight your capabilities in order to get that job. The interviewer also seeks to learn more about you, something illuminating that couldn't be put into the résumé. This question is not about just building a rapport with you. Through this question, which most interviewers choose to begin the session with, they also seek to analyze how the candidates handle themselves in a stressful situation, the level of the confidence the candidates project as well as the level of their articulacy. This question is created with the purpose of unhinging the interviewee, as prepared as they may be, to get an understanding of what the interviewees categorize as important to them.

Remember that this is your chance to bring out the brilliant side of you for the interviewer to know and you must make good of this opportunity to shine as the most likely-to-be hired among the list of candidates. Do not employ modesty and downplay your own performance. Be prepared to answer this question by focusing on your strengths and the interviewers' interests, and positively describe yourself to the interviewer. Plan out a response that best demonstrates who you are, your qualifications and experience and how they contribute to making you suitable for the job, along with your own personal interests in applying for this job. Keep it short and precise as you will have to summarize it all within a minute or two.

Since this question is likely to be the first question that is posed to you after the initial introductions, whatever response you offer will set the tone for the rest of the interview and can either make it or break it for you.

The key considerations here are:

- Did you convey your interest in the job with optimism and interest?

- Did you project yourself in a positive light?

- Did you struggle to respond and let your confidence slip?

Given below is a walkthrough on how you can handle the *"Tell me about yourself"* query:

Stay calm throughout the interview

Maintain your composure and keep your thoughts collected while you answer to the query. Although it is easier said than done, you can achieve this calmness if you practice beforehand about what you are going to say along with techniques to calm yourself. Plan your words without any vague examples or references and try out different ways of answering the question until you find the one that satisfies you the most. During the interview session, relay your responses in a thoughtful and precise manner. Talk about yourself, your work and your expectations with this job. Try not to stumble early in the interview otherwise, you may lose your momentum and composure. And do not ramble about your personal matters, hobbies or preferences and irrelevant history of work.

Don't recite your résumé

The interviewers will have your résumé in front of them, so don't give complete readout or a complete breakdown of it as they may have already read most or some part of it. To them, you will only be repeating what is set before them and what they already gathered rather than what they seek to discover from you. This, in turn, will show your lack of preparation as well as the poorness of your skill in communicating with others. You can address the vital achievements that you have put in your résumé but make sure they are relevant to the job post you have applied for. Give the interviewer a format by which they can question you further about yourself; provide them with additional information rather than restricting them to the points in your résumé.

Focus on what the Interviewer wants

To begin with, you need to understand that the Interviewer wants to know the professional side of you rather than know you as a person. If you need to know what the interviewer wants to know about you or what his interest is in, look no further than the requirements of the job; convince the interviewer that you are the right person for this job and that you cannot just do it, but do it well. You need to tell them that you are capable of fitting in their team and growing with them, in experience, all as a result of your previous experiences and accomplishments. Craft your response in accordance with the concerns of the employer.

Focus on your primary strengths

Keep a clear idea of your key strengths as these will be your selling points in an interview. From your leadership skills to problem-solving capabilities, you must list all your strengths that will be effective for handling the job role and will give you the advantage in acquiring the job. If asked, you can briefly explain the stories that define your strengths to convey to the interviewer that it is genuine. The quality of your skill set and qualifications must agree with the requirements of the job. If you are applying for a team leader, then you must be the one to take initiatives as well as carry out successful coordination and communication, not only among the members of your team, but with the leaders of another teams too. If the job post is for customer service, then you may want to highlight your role in driving the sales of the products as well as handling customer complaints.

Explain your interest

You can easily explain your interest in the job post if you have keenly done your research and understood how well the requirements of the company and the job sit with your own qualifications, experience and acquired skill set. Express to the interviewer how you can contribute to this job and the company. Tell him how you expect to be benefited by this job post and through this company. Choose your words wisely to show your enthusiasm and not your desperation, and make it sound genuine too. Avoid making a reference to your personal issues for the need to have this job; keep it career oriented and explain how this job could be a challenge you are ready to accept to enhance your capability and broaden your responsibilities.

Describe your background

Talking about your professional background is essential to let the interviewer understand how you have evolved professionally. Make sure you keep a verbal flow that concurs with the job you are applying for. Show them how your previous job/jobs have helped you prepare for this switch in career. And if you are starting out in the job market, then explain how your qualification, the courses and extracurricular activities you have taken have trained you to become eligible for this post. Show them that you are a determined, flexible and hard working person; prove that you qualify for the position and company, by talking about the years of your previous work or training experience.

Be careful when expressing other interests

Talking about your hobbies will give the interviewer insight on you as an individual and they will form an opinion of who they think you are. So focus on hobbies that are relevant and beneficial to personal and professional growth and development. You can mention hobbies such as playing sports which will show your competitive spirit and team work , reading books (lifetime learner), volunteer work in the community are just a few examples of hobbies that will leave a favorable impression with the interviewer. You can specify interests like learning other languages, taking short courses in emerging technology that could directly benefit your work.

Show off your achievements

Don't shy from listing off your major accomplishments if they are not already listed in your résumé. Your interviewer wants to hear about what sets you apart and what you bring to the table, so briefly explain to the interviewer how you managed to gain that success. Make sure that your key achievements fit in with the job position you have applied for, or highlights your capability and skill set required for this job without sounding irrelevant. If you are applying for a job where customers are prioritized, show them how you handled customer complaints successfully. If you are a salesperson, then explain how you helped exceed the goals for sales of the product. Primarily, show them how adaptable and flexible you are in a work environment; how you aim to exceed the expectations of your superiors and be an active and supporting team player.

Avoid asking for clarifications

Do not answer this question with "What would you like to know?" This clearly shows your lack of preparation and gives vibes of indifference from you to the interviewer. Come prepared with your response and deliver it effectively before you question the interviewer about any other information they may require, else wait for them to pose further questions to you.

Show them that hiring you is not a mistake

Give your interviewer a best representation of yourself. Give them enough reasons to base a decision positively in your favor. Remember that as a hiring personnel, they will be critical in their assessment of you as their choice of selection will reflect back to them and they wouldn't want to hire someone who puts their reputation on the line. Show them your willingness to work for the company and adapt to its environment. Avoid mentioning any stories about any disagreements within your previous workplaces as this throws a negative light on you.

Now that you have an idea of what you are going to say, plan out your statements accordingly. But there must be an order to how you say it all; you cannot just randomly leap from one point to another. For example, following up your introduction with your interest in the job post and then your qualifications, or jumping back to a previous statement because you forgot to mention something of relevance. You need to show them you are well-prepared not clumsy.

Given below is a strategy of how to structure your response:

Who you are: –

You first statement must be an introduction of your professional self - who you are and what you do at present. Do not mention where and how you grew up and with how many members of your family as this classifies as irrelevant information. Make this statement about who you are as a job applicant. Express your role and the years of your experience. Follow it up with what you do or did for the company (make sure to mention the name of the company you worked for) as an active employee and also who you work for or with. Make sure to keep it all in a positive light else it could reflect your negativity.

Your key expertise: –

Talk about your past work experiences and the skills you accomplished through them. Focus on your experiences and performances. Do not make it elaborate, starting with your first job to the last one. Instead, make it interesting and impressive by focusing on the areas that have helped you grow professionally. Simplify it with a template that addresses your challenge, how you dealt with it and what the final result was. If you can, quantify your results in percentages or budget. Make a humble mention of any awards or certificates or promotions you may have achieved during this time. Talk about your role as a team player. Avoid giving off an impression that you weren't positive about your career path.

Why this job: –

Finish by telling the interviewer about your interest in the job and company and why you want the position. Express to them what plans you have for the company and how you hope to make it better through this job. Prove to them that you have indeed invested your time and done your research regarding the company and that your own goals align with those of the company. Don't get candid about problems with your previous employers or workplace. Keep it concise and simple, focusing on how this job can offer you a challenge you are ready to accept and grow with. Be genuine with your words and express your interest in this job.

Plan out your statement and practice well before you walk in for the interview. You must clearly understand what to say and what not to say in your mind as you work it out and stick to the proper flow of words to avoid any incoherence and cause the hiring manager to tune out during the interview.

Effectively utilize this open-ended question to your benefit by crafting each response in such a way that you stand out from the list of applicants for the interviewer. Keep it professionally informative and interesting enough to compel the interviewer to hire you.

To summarize, here's how you can answer the 'tell me about yourself' question:

What to say?

- ✓ Work experience
- ✓ Skill set that fits with the job

- ✓ Your interest in the job

- ✓ Your achievements

What not to say?

- o Personal information

- o Irrelevant hobbies

- o Breakdown of resume

It's time to stop dreading and getting sweaty palms at the idea of answering this question. Take down your notes and put together an impressive response for your interview day. Wow the hiring managers with your confidence, articulacy and belief in yourself.

CHAPTER 3

WHAT EMPLOYERS WANT TO HEAR FROM JOB SEEKERS

A great resume can get you an interview, but knowing what your employer wants can increase your chances of receiving the job offer. As we have seen earlier, it is necessary to understand what the hiring managers want to hear from you to differentiate you from the list of other job applicants. Deciphering these elements can be easy only if you know what to look for and how to look. Your only key here is preparation.

The initial and the essential step in the preparation is to research the organization and the job position offered. This gives you the idea of what is expected of you as a job applicant. The next equally important step is to craft your answers to their requirements in a way that enable you to sell yourself.

Listed below are the skills that hiring managers wish to decipher from your statements when interviewing you for the job:

10 KEYS ON HOW TO SUCCESSFULLY SELL YOUR TALENT, SKILLS, AND ABILITIES

I am aware of the Organization

Show the hiring personnel that you have done your research concerning the company, its policies, and objectives, that you have invested your time in doing this homework to understand who you might be working for and who they are and what they want to be. Show them you are passionate about this job and are well aware of the missions and goals of the company. Look into the company's weaknesses and strengths as this could give you the idea whether you wish to work for them or not. Else, contribute to their development in some way with your skill set. Demonstrate this knowledge by asking the right questions during the interview or expressing your interest in working with them.

I am a problem solver

Every company wants an employee who has the ability to look at the problem and analyze it accurately in order to contrive effective solutions. An innovative approach to problem solving is also highly appreciated. Provide the knowledge of your problem-solving abilities to the interviewer by detailing about the projects you have worked on and how you crafted solutions for them.

I am highly motivated

Proving yourself as a self-motivated person is essential to the hiring process. Most hiring managers seek this attribute among the candidates as this portrays their commitment to the job, their willingness to work on their own without prodding and how they can be a productive addition to the team. Self-motivation is one trait that cannot be taught and must come from the candidate. Employers need candidates that don't require constant supervision and reminders from their managers but are simply enthusiastic about their job. Show them that once you get your instructions, you will get the job done to the best of your abilities.

I am flexible

You need to show your flexibility in the workplace. Employers expect you to be flexible to the job as this shows your ability to adapt to any scenario within the job. You need to show them you are not difficult to work with and can flex yourself with the job and company's requirements, whether it is a shift in the work schedule or change of client site or even changes in technology. Prove to them that you fit into their work environment and culture.

I am a team player

You need to demonstrate to the interviewer that you are a team player, that you are capable of keeping the goals of the team before your own. A team player exhibits many qualities that are appreciated in the workplace: communication, reliability, adaptability, etc. Highlight the strength of your team and how you actively contributed and offered reliable support to it. Do not downplay the role of your team but highlight your own effectiveness, how you adapted to the role and how you contributed to meeting the deadlines.

I have excellent soft skills

Convince the interviewer that you have the right soft skills to effectively contribute to the job and work team. Communication is an important aspect of any job. Show the interviewer that you are an effective communicator; only by listening carefully, understanding well and speaking effectively can get you the job. Present yourself as respectful, positive and confident during the interview.

Listen carefully to what they say and genuinely respond, or inquire according to the knowledge given to you. Brief your work experience to show how organized, dependable and motivated you stay, even under work pressure.

I am optimistic

Give the hiring personnel the best attitude: from the moment you arrive at the venue for the interview to the moment you leave the venue, maintain a friendly, polite and confident personality with everyone you interact. Shake hands with your interviewers and address them with lots of smiles and maintain eye contact throughout the interview. Don't address them by their first names unless you are asked to. Show them that you are pleasant to work with and can be a positive influence and addition to the team. They need to know that you are an agreeable person and you tend to resolve issues rather than create conflicts and challenge others.

I am an active learner

Impress your interviewer with your growth mindset, show them that you seek to grow professionally through your work responsibilities and the company that hires you more than your personal advancement. Displaying traits that convey to them your interest in constantly learning and improving your skills shows your flexibility and adaptability. Tell them how you have evolved in your previous assignments goaded by your innate thirst to learn and do better. Use this as an indicator of your future performance – the hiring managers need to know what you can offer to the job, how you can contribute to the company's growth.

I can add value to the organization

In the end, it all comes down to what you are willing to offer, how and by how much you are ready to contribute to the growth of the organization. Tell them what you can do to advance the company towards its organizational goals and objectives. Present yourself as an invaluable candidate by listing all your attributes that are in agreement with this job.

I am inquisitive and passionate about what I do

Nothing gets this point across better than the questions you pose during the interview about the job, its requirements, and the company. Show them you are interested, not only in your own goals but that of the company too.

Prove to them that you have done the research and have the right set of questions for them in return. Don't be shy or indifferent and ask them about the job and the company. Although, avoid asking questions about salary and whether or not you will get the job.

Give the hiring managers just what they crave – an employee who fits in with the company. As ever, you need to prepare yourself to present the best and professional version of you. Take note of these keys to respond according to the needs of the company and the interviewer and successfully sell your talents to get that job offer.

CHAPTER 4

TOP TEN QUESTIONS TO ASK AT A JOB INTERVIEW

Even though an interview may seem like a unilateral interaction where the hiring manager ceaselessly interrogates you and you try to come up with best responses in order to get hired, it is meant to serve as a dialogue where the two of you try to arrive at a conclusion that is mutually beneficial. From the interviewer's point of view, they need an employee that is enthusiastic about the job and as such is willing to fit in with the company's environment. While they have their own set of reasons to make inquiries that seem relevant to them, you too as an interviewee should have your own set of questions prepared. Interviews are not just about the employers and your need to present the best of you before them; as a job aspirant, you must be aware of how this job and company can affect your career, for the better of course. During the end of the interview, take this chance to make your own inquiries to help you evaluate the job and decide if it is the right one for you.

Be sure to maintain a friendly tone and positive attitude when you shift the focus to the interviewer and the company. Prepare your list of questions not only before you go in for the interview, but register any information that the employer offers you during the interview and re-design your questions around them.

Given below are the top ten questions that you as a possible employee should ask in an interview:

The Job

Question #1:

- Can you give me details about the enjoyable and challenging aspects of this job?

- What can be the biggest challenges someone in this job would probably have to face?

- Show the interviewer that you are positively interested in this role and even though you are anticipating facing the challenges, you'd like to have an idea of what they are. This shows that you are very well-prepared to be hired.

Question #2:

- What parts of this role are satisfying for successful people in this industry/company?

- What qualities should someone possess to be successful in this job role?

- Demonstrate to the interviewer that you are not only focused on being successful but also successfully fulfill your role. Follow up this question after mentioning some aspects or attributes that the interviewer might have mentioned earlier to display your excellent listening skills.

Question #3:

- Can you explain to me how the role is integrated into the organization and how it affects overall the structure of it?

- What company goals are you primarily focusing on for now, and how does the team work and offer support in effectively advancing towards those objectives?

This question expresses your willingness to work as a part of a team to effectively contribute to the company. It shows your interest in clearly understanding your role, how the role is integrated into the company, its affiliations and expected contribution and how it would eventually affect the overall company.

Question #4:

- Is there any opportunities for promotion in the future in this job role?

- This question shows your ability to be goal-oriented and determination to make progress on your work.

Training

Question #5:

- What are the different types of training opportunities your company offers to new employees?

- What kind of training programs has the company made available to the employees?

- Is there a possibility for professional advancement and development under the guidance of the company?

Use this question to highlight your interest in keeping up with the knowledge and advancing your skills. Companies look for employees who are active learners and want to contribute to the company's growth.

The Work culture

Question #6:

- Can you please tell me about the work environment here?

- What can you tell me about the work culture here? Are the employees collaborative in their approach or do they prefer the independent style of work?

- How was the last team event? Can you tell me about it?

- Can I get an idea about the company's environment and the culture? How do the teams integrate and contribute to it?

This question too conveys your passion for working with a team, but at the same time expresses your need to work in a positive and cooperative environment to be able to give the best you have got to offer and with complete efficiency.

Performance

Question #7:

- ❖ How do you measure and review the performance

of the employees?

- ❖ What initial expectations concerning performance can I anticipate from your side for this job role?

- ❖ What is the measure of success in your company and how do you evaluate it?

- ❖ Can you tell me about the metrics, goals or any other measure against which an employees' performance is evaluated here?

This question ensures the interviewer that you value work commitment, you are reliable and appreciate the importance of delivering results with optimal efficiency at the least, and with regard to the deadlines.

The Company / Organization

Question #8:

- • What issues are the primary concerns of your company? Or what issues do you expect the company could be facing in the next year?

- • I gathered that the company has recently introduced a new [X: product, service, etc.] How has it benefited the organization so far and what more is expected from it?

- Can you please detail me about the new products the company has launched? What are the company's plans for its growth?

These variations both show that you are interested in the job as well as the company. Make it obviously clear to the interviewer that you have done some research on the company's interests regarding their newly introduced product, service, project or division; made your own evaluation, and you are now eager to get their point of view regarding these matters.

Self

Question #9:

- Would you like me to tell you more about my interests in [X]?

- Would you like to know anything else regarding [X]?

- Do you have any other questions for me?

When talking about yourself, you can be cheeky or polite and pose a direct question with the focus on your talents, such as meeting with clients, handling customers concerns and complaints, introducing and developing innovative products, implementing better technology and systems. Or you can inquire if the interviewer has any further questions to ask you.

Question #10:

- Do you have any doubts about my background and how can I be suited to this position?

- What level of skills and experience are you expecting for this job role?

- Do you think I am well suited for this role?

Again, you can be brazen in emphasizing your skills and strengths and show that you are open to constructive criticism to improve yourself. Also, you can inquire about their expectations and as such address your willingness to improve.

CHAPTER 5

12 SMART GETTING HIRED QUESTIONS TO ASK DURING AN INTERVIEW

As stated in the previous chapter, an interview is a two-way interaction and it is your task to make it so. While your questions must help you decide if this job and all that comes with it is suitable for you, they must also make you seem observant and smart. Show the interviewer that you are interested in this job, for mutual benefit, and that you have prepared for it too by doing your bit of research.

Design your questions around the job, the department, the company and the industry. Conduct your research and make notes on these topics and any other that interest you. Keep them focused yet open-ended.

Thus, at the end of the interview, when the employer says, "Do you have any questions for us?" be sure to demonstrate your interest – and intelligence – through your inquiries.

Given below are some sample questions that you can ask and make an impression:

(You don't need to fire all these questions in one go; chances are some of them will be covered during the entire course of the interview. So, stay observant and choose the ones that best convey your interest and answer any other doubts that you may have.)

Question#1:

- ❖ What are the day-to-day responsibilities of someone holding this job position?

- ❖ Can I have a walkthrough of a typical day in this role?

- ❖ Are the primary responsibilities for this position expected to change in the next few months or year?

Make sure that you have a clear idea of what the job role entails, what is expected of you and how likely is it to change over the course. Learn as much as possible about the job role so that this information can help you decide if this is the job for you, should you be extended the offer. Inquiring about the daily tasks that are involved in the job will give you an insight into the skills that you may need. In case this has already been covered, questions about the possibility that the responsibilities for the job would change over time and what that change would involve.

Question#2

- ❖ What ideally successful qualities do you expect a candidate to have in order to undertake this role?

- ❖ What skills are you hoping the new hire will possess in order to make the team complete?

This sort of question can often help you to acquire valuable information that is not in the job description. It can also help you learn about the environment of the company as well as their expectations of this role, so you express how well suited you are.

Question#3:

- Are there any significant immediate projects that need to be completed?

- Can I have an idea of the projects that I will be

undertaking in this job position?

Inquire about the projects that the company expects this job role to immediately address. This question portrays your interest and concern in the industry that the company is focused on.

Question#4:

- What plans does the organization have for the company in the next few years?

- What exciting milestones can I anticipate in the company's future?

- It is necessary to make sure that the company is growing and the current employees are well established in their role to see that happen.

Question#5:

- Who is the greatest competitor to the company and why?

- How different is this company from all the other competitors?

You should gather this information during your research and know about the company's major competitors, but it is useful to the interviewer for their views as they will be able to give you the insight you can't find anywhere else. You can further the discussion based on your knowledge and inquire what sets them apart from their own point of view.

Question#6:

- Currently, are there any immediate problems that need to be addressed and solved within your department?

Show your desire to seize an opportunity as a self-starter and problem-solver and learn about the company's immediate focus for the next several months.

Question#7:

- Does the company have any major challenges to face at the moment?

Inquire about the immediate challenges the company may be facing at the moment: what trends do they need to incorporate and what are the issues they are facing in order to advance in the industry. This will help you make your decision in undertaking the job and determining where and how you can focus your strengths for the betterment of the company.

Question#8:

- Can I ask you about the best part of working for this company?

- Can I inquire when and why did you come to this company?

Asking about the interviewer's personal experience cannot only help you build rapport but also gain insight into the company's culture.

Question#9:

- Can you explain the general career path for someone in this job role?

- Will I be provided any training for this position?

By asking the question, you show your interest in growing along with the organization. Inquire about the promotions and the training involved during the career.

Question#10:

- What do you like about my background and experience compared to the other candidates that you have interviewed?

- How would you describe an ideal candidate for

this role? How do I compare with them?

If things are going well and you managed to build a good rapport, this question will help you visualize if there are issues that you could address to prove why you are the best person for the role. Positively take the response from the interviewer.

Question#11:

- What can you tell me about the team that I would be working with in this position?

- Who am I supposed to interact with regularly in this position?

- Who can I address my reports to?

- What other departments are most likely to interact with this role?

Inquiring about the team shows your interest in working as a team member and your acknowledgment of collaboration and respect among the team members.

Question#12:

- Can you tell me about the next steps in the interview process?

Show that you are eager to move forward in the interviewing process. Inquire about the timeline for hiring so that you can follow up appropriately.

CHAPTER 6

HOW TO SUCCESSFULLY ANSWER TOUGH QUESTIONS AND GET HIRED

105 Questions and Answers You Need to Know for a Successful Job Interview

In any job interview, you may encounter several questions. The key to deciphering how to best respond to the question is in knowing what type of a question it is, and then quickly working up a response that the interviewer will very likely want to hear. In any given interview, there will be the following types of questions:

- Directive questions

- Non-directive questions

- Behavioral and Hypothetical questions

- Industry/Company related questions

- Stress questions

Directive questions: These types of questions are normally clear and specific and are based on your résumé.

— 55 —

Non-Directive questions: They are open-ended and less structured questions that allow you to talk about yourself.

Behavioral questions: These are the very commonly asked questions that are designed to assess how you respond in under specific circumstances, given your previous experience. These questions are posed to ask you how you reacted in a particular situation.

Hypothetical questions: They are similar to the behavioral questions, only they are aimed to assess how you are likely to respond to a particular issue in the future.

Industry or Company related questions: If you state that you have researched the company and job then you are very likely to be asked such questions regarding various aspects of the company. Otherwise, the interviewer will still ask you questions related to the company and the industry to figure out if you have done your research.

Stress questions: Interviewers employ these type of questions to assess how candidates react without adequate preparation. These questions can at times sound dumb but are designed to assess your ability to think on your feet. They generally don't have a right or wrong answer.

Other types of questions are technical and involve you to exhibit your skill sets. Some competitive and high-profile companies make use of questions with more sophisticated forms of logical reasoning to test the level of your skills. These questions are random and are designed to analyze your craft in forming logical and mathematical solutions to resolve a problem.

Here are 105 Job Interview Questions and Answers You Need to Know about Getting Hired that have been classified into the 6 types of interview questions:

Directive Interview Questions

Directive interview questions are clear and require a precise response from you as they are generally based on the information you have provided in your résumé. If you are well aware of your abilities and have designed the résumé accordingly, then these questions should be fairly simple for you to answer.

The best way to answer these questions is by being honest about your work experience and by backing up your answers with your work: what you have done in the current or previous job and how you have done it. Some questions will require you to answer with a yes or a no, following it up with a plausible explanation without having the interviewer ask you why. Explain to the interviewer how your current skill and experiences set avails you to be the best candidate for this job.

Given below are the sample questions and how best you can respond to them.

Question #1:

Can you describe your work experience for me?

Answer: Hiring managers use this question to assess your personal feelings about your work. Through your description, they will analyze how you feel about your work. You can respond by saying your work was either satisfying and helped you achieve your target or you can state that it is challenging, but refrain from making any negative statements about it. You do not want to come off as weak and unmotivated to the interviewer.

Question #2:

How does your work experience prepare you for the responsibilities of this position?

Tell me to what extent your education equips you for this job?

How do you think your educational / work background prepares you for this role?

Can you tell me how your experience matches the job description?

Answer: In order to respond appropriately to this question, you should have a clear idea of the requirements of this job as well as your own skill set derived from your experiences. Using a few examples which highlight your skill sets that are pertinent to this post, express to the interviewer how your past training has made you eligible for this post. Show them that this job is the next phase in your personal growth and you are ready to undertake this challenge.

Question #3:

Can you work as a part of a team?

Answer: You need to show your passion for working in agreement with other team members, and how best you can contribute to the team in a specific role. There is only one answer to this question: Yes; support this claim with examples. Any other response would very likely not get you the job offer.

Question #4:

Answer: Can you tell us about your résumé?

Have a clear idea of your resume and memorize it, even to the last moment updates that you have made. Chances are the interviewer would ask you to explain your resume. Your response will show to the interviewer how serious you are about this job and that you have indeed taken care to prepare your resume.

Question #5:

Are you quick at learning new things?

Are you interested in learning?

Answer: This question requires you to be truthful regarding your speed of learning. Some jobs require you to update yourself with the new things in demand and learn about them as early as you can. For example, there are jobs with customer service that frequently keep updating for ensuring customer satisfaction. If you take time in learning things, then you may not be able to keep up with the pace of the job.

Question #6:

How well can you handle a computer?

What kinds of equipment can you operate?

Answer: In the present day, you must have a working knowledge of how to use a computer if you aim to get hired for a job. You must have proper knowledge of computers, how to use them, and the different applications and software that are installed. If you have prior training in software and hardware fixing, then do state it as it will be taken in your favor.

If your work experience has enabled to you tackle any other types of equipment that are used for the job you are applying for, then make a mention of those too.

Question #7:

How fast can you type?

What is your typing speed?

Answer: If your job post requires you to note inquiries or take notes of the meetings or client requirements, then you need to have a fast typing speed. Again, be honest with your response.

Question #8:

Do you have an active social profile?

Answer: In this present age, your activity on social media tells a lot about you. Many companies expect you to be socially active these days and maintain an impressive presence on the online social media. This help enhance the image of the company and make any other promotional adverts effective.

Question #9:

Do you have any difficulty in socializing with people from other backgrounds?

Answer: Within a company, if there are people from various backgrounds, societies, races and ethnicities, then you can be inquired about your comfort in working there. You have to be clear in stating that you don't believe in things like racism even though you know they exist. You can tell about your many different friends from various races and ethnicities if you have any.

Question #10:

Will it be alright with you if we reached out to your previous employers?

Answer: Sometimes, the hiring managers would call your previous employers to know about you. At other times, they ask this question only to imply that they might contact your former employer and make further inquiries about you. This question can solely be for the purpose of inquiry or it could be a trick employed by the interviewer to get you to be honest. Confidently reply with a yes, but it is always preferable to have good relations with your other employers.

Question #11:

Are you able to easily multitask?

Answer: Be upfront about how many tasks you can handle at once; if you say yes, then it is expected that you will perform every task with perfection and full efficiency. Some jobs may require you to multitask but not everyone can be great at multitasking. If you cannot deliver each task with the expected results, then you won't be considered a multitasker.

Question #12:

Do you consider yourself as an organized person?

Answer: Considering a work environment, the only response you can give to the interviewer is one that is satisfactory. Tell the interviewer how organized you are by stating your daily schedule and how you plan out your tasks during the day.

Question #13:

Do you keep yourself updated with the changes in your field of work?

Answer: Employers expect you to stay updated with the field and industry you are working for as this shows that you are not just someone who works for the salary but are actively employed and passionate about your job and have your career goals set. Replying with a yes will require you to show them how updated you are.

Question #14:

Can you tell me for how long have you been unemployed? Can I ask you why?

Answer: Your resume will pretty much speak for you in response to this query. However, if you have a genuine reason, then clearly state it. Refrain from making any witty statements.

Question #15:

I see that you worked for a particular employer for a very long time. Can I inquire why?

Answer: If there is a particular employer on your resume that you have worked with for a long time, you will face this question. Talk about how great a relationship you had with your previous employer, their attitude, and how it all eventually contributed to your personal growth and achievements.

Question #16:

Why do you want to change your career?

Answer: If you had to change your career path in the middle, then you have to be ready to face this question. However, you can always explain your maturity as a professional. You can also explain how your previous work experience led you to realize that you would be good for this change of career.

Question #17:

Would you prefer making the decisions on your own?

Answer: The response to this question depends on whether or not you are a team player and what you stated concerning that. If you are a team player, then it is unlikely that you will be making the decisions alone.

Question #18:

Have you ever been criticized? Do you think you can you handle criticism?

How do you react to any criticism?

Answer: In a professional environment, it is expected of you to take criticism and use it to your advantage rather than getting upset about it. You might be asked to quote that one instance when you had to take criticism. You will also be inquired how you dealt with the criticism.

Question #19:

Would you like to tell us about something else we may have missed?

Answer: If you really think that there is something about your career, experience, and personality that should be highlighted but no questions were asked about it, then state that particular thing in response to this question. It will show your confidence.

Question #20:

Would you like to inquire about something?

Do you have any questions of your own?

Answer: It is better if you save some questions to ask your interviewer. You could even ask confidently if the interviewer liked your answers and your personality, but you must be prepared for any response that comes your way.

The sole purpose of the interviewer in querying you with such directive questions is to relate to your experiences – of education, work and elsewhere – and analyze how it all eventually adds up to your ability to perform the job.

NonDirective Interview Questions

Nondirective interview questions are open-ended and flexible, giving you the opportunity to showcase your strengths and experiences. These general questions allow you the freedom to determine the focus of your answers as the interviewer does not seek specific answers but an assessment of you as an eligible candidate.

Though, do not take liberty in answering such questions as you wish; your focus must be in highlighting your abilities and proving to the interviewer what makes you eligible for the job. Cover your education, experiences, skills and attributes as per the job requirement in the response you give. Use these questions to effectively sell your talents to the interviewer. The most common nondirective query is the "Tell me about yourself."

Follow the sample questions given below to understand what you could be facing:

Question #21:

Please introduce yourself.

Can you tell us a little about yourself?

Answer: This is the most commonly asked question in any interview and falls under the category of nondirective question. You are expected to sum up your qualifications, work experience, achievements and business goals within a minute or two. Make sure every word you say counts and your response is relevant and concise. Since this question is very likely to be the first thing you are asked in an interview, this is your only chance to set the pace. Put forth your skill set and explain how it makes you eligible for the job in question. Preparation for this question is crucial to the success of the interview.

Question #22:

How was your last job experience?

What was your previous job like?

Answer: Give a concise and positive reply to this question. Do not come off as angry or negative about your ex-employer, the workplace or your previous job. And refrain from mentioning any issues you may have had with them. If you believe that your last job was not offering you the challenge you needed or was not related to your skills, then state it as confidently and clearly as you can without maligning your previous boss or company.

Question #23:

Can you tell me why would you like to work here?

Answer: Craft a response that makes you sound intelligent and interesting. Avoid getting too candid with your response. Frankly stating that you are here for the money or being cordial and saying that it is a nice place for work will not boost your character. Your answers could be precise and honest, but they are certainly not what the hiring manager wants to hear in this case as they only highlight what you want for yourself. Plus, it will demonstrate your lack of actual preparation. Instead, opt for a professional approach by stating how your experience in the field made you think that you were suitable for this position. Make it about the company and how you think you can contribute to it, rather than stating the obvious of how you expect to be benefited. You will be expected to mention how you found the job posting too.

Question #24:

Why do you think you are fit for this role?

Answer: This is a very crucial question and your response to this question can have a huge impact on your selection or rejection. To boost yourself, you would want to mention your experience, skills, and qualification. Tell the interviewer how your qualifications and experience are perfectly in line with the technical skills required for the position you are applying for and draw on examples from when you have used your skills in a practical scenario. Make them realize that you understand the company and its work, products and objectives. At the same time, make sure to bring out your passion and enthusiasm for the job and other aspects of that role, for example, the technologies involved.

Question #25:

Can you explain why do you want to work for us?

Answer: Regardless of you having taken your time

to apply for the job and appear for an interview, the interviewer can still ask you to describe why you want to work for them at some point during the interview. There are many ways to respond to this question, but the one you must say is the one that defines clearly how you think the company can help with your growth and in return what you hope to achieve for the company. Talk about how the company's objectives or environment (as you have gathered from your research) excites you and thus, what privileges you hope to achieve through them. Tie it up with how you think your own experience can be beneficial to the company's own growth and value.

Question #26:

Can you tell me about your strengths?

What do you consider your professional strengths?

What do you think makes you unique?

Answer: The interviewer wants to know the quality of your personality, which directly contributes to your professional work, makes you better than all the other job applicants and how confident you are about it. You have to figure out that one trait in you that is relevant to the job position and makes you a great professional, and sell it to the interviewer. It is best if you have an example gained from your experience to back your claim. Take care to be accurate with your claim and not mention something you think the interviewer wants to hear.

Question #27:

What are your weaknesses?

What do you consider as your greatest professional weakness?

Answer: Similar to your personal strengths, the interviewer seeks to know about your professional weaknesses (not your physical weaknesses), to identify any major issues with your level of professionalism. Take care not to state too many of them and do not talk about anything that makes you appear as a rude or non-professional person. Tell them why you think it is your weakness and also how you are trying to overcome it and improve your caliber. This question serves as a gauge of your self-awareness and level of honesty for the interviewer.

Question #28:

Can you talk about the biggest accomplishment you have had in your career?

What do you consider as your greatest professional achievement?

Answer: This question is crucial in making the interviewer more interested in hiring you, owing to your record of achieving amazing results in past jobs. Your response to this question tells them that you have done your job to the best of your capabilities. It will also help them understand what the idea of a biggest accomplishment is to you. Brief the interviewer on the situation and the task you were required to complete and then detail out what you did, how you did it and in the end, what results were achieved.

Question #29:

Tell us about a conflict that you might have had at some previous job.

Answer: This question is used to analyze your problem-solving abilities in a conflicting situation. Detail the interviewer about a conflict you may have had on the previous job and make sure to talk about the way you professionally handled that matter.

Question #30:

How do you cope with work pressure?

Answer: This question is used to assess your ability to stay focused in a conflicting situation Present the interviewer with an example of how you handled pressure on a previous occasion. But make sure not to talk about the bad decisions you may have made under the pressure.

Question #31:

How much do you rate yourself on a scale of 10?

Answer: The interviewers will ask you this question if they want to know how insightful and well aware you are of your capabilities and get an idea of how you perceive yourself, and the level of confidence you have in your abilities. Professionals who have a high level of confidence are greatly admired by companies and hiring managers because confident people perform at their optimum efficiency; they are highly productive and make better decisions. If you are fully convinced of your capabilities, then you had better rate yourself higher and say that you are getting even better with time.

Question #32:

What were your favorite subjects as a student? Why?

Answer: List out the subjects that you were most

interested in during your time as a student, along with reasons. You might even have to mention the subjects you didn't like as much. However, make sure that it does not conflict with your job requirements in any case as the employer may likely induce that you may underperform with that regard or wholly lose your interest.

Question #33:

What drove you to your choice of the major subject?

Answer: In response to this query, explain to the interviewer your choice of the major subject along with solid reasons: why you were interested in beginning with, rather than responding that you found it easy.

Question #34:

Do you have a vision or mission statement?

Answer: Having a personal mission and vision will tell the interviewer that you are indeed serious about your career and profession; that you are proactively guiding your career and well aware of who you want to be, what you want to do and where you wish to be in your career. Prepare your mission and vision statements well in advance and keep them concise when inquired, if you take too much time in stating it to the interviewer, you will make it clear that you don't have any personal goals.

Question #35:

As part of a team, how will / do you motivate others?

Answer: If you apply for a job that requires you to be a part of a team, or you state your ability to be a contributing team member, the interviewer will very likely ask about your methods for motivating your co-team members. Truthfully respond to this question of how you offer your support to others in the team. Professionally state how you stay in touch with other members of the team, listen to everyone, how you acknowledge their strengths and weaknesses while assigning them to the proper roles and encourage them to tackle their issues.

Question #36:

Can you anticipate problems well in advance or do you comfortably handle them as they arise?

Answer: The interviewer seeks to understand how insightful you are of the matters you are dealing with: whether you are already aware of the problems you will be dealing with or you hope to tackle them as they come. Your answer depends on the requirement of the job: if you are applying for an analyst or managerial posts, then anticipating a problem would be the best response. Tell the interviewer whether your observational skills help you in foreseeing the problem or you are more suited to reacting to the issue and tackling it as it manifests. You can provide support with an example from your previous employers.

Question #37:

Do you think you can be an ideal manager?

Answer: This question is mostly asked if you are looking for a managerial position in a company as a gauge of your success in such a role. Through this question, the interviewer seeks to understand your perception of leadership and how you handle the responsibility of management. Tell them how you get the job done and how you handle the people involved in the work with you.

Question #38:

Can you describe what sort of person you would like to work for?

What is your ideal employer like?

Answer: Through your response, the interviewer seeks to identify what you see as a perfect employer and how their organization fits your description – if they don't fit with your idea of "ideal", it is highly likely that they wouldn't hire you, expecting you not to comfortably fit in with the employer. It's better to avoid getting into details and being too precise with your answer. You response also reveals what sort of a manager you will likely be.

Question #39:

How do you think the work environment can be improved to make it ideal for employees?

Answer: Even though it seems as if the interviewer wants to talk about the rights of the employees, your response will have to be limited, bearing in mind the costs of employing such improvements. Talk about maintaining a good relationship between the employer and the employee as a support pillar for a successful work environment.

Question #40:

Are you interviewing at some other companies?

What other companies are you interviewing with?

Answer: If you are attending an interview in one company, it is very likely that you are looking elsewhere too. The response to this question allows the interviewer to judge your seriousness for the job as well as the competition they could be facing. It is best to mention you are indeed exploring other options in the industry and seeking the opportunity to apply your skills to new challenges.

Behavioral And Hypothetical Interview Questions

Certain nondirective questions are aimed at assessing your behavioral and problem-solving capabilities in order to determine how you will perform at your job. These come under the behavioral and hypothetical interview questions. These questions are aimed at understanding your story – your professional story – and each story is derived based on the bullets in your résumé. This kind of questions asks you to explain how you did or would react to a particular scenario. You need self-awareness and an approach that provides direct answers as to how you think and how you behave and indirectly tell the interviewer what you want, keeping in mind what the interviewer seeks to hear from you.

Behavioral Questions: The interviewer assesses your job performance based on how you have tackled an issue in the past: they are inclined to believe that what you did in the past is an indicator of how you will respond in the future. Such questions generally begin with "How did you handle/manage ... in the past?" and include a situation that is relatively similar to the job description.

There is no specific answer to this question, but you have to relate it to the skills and qualities required for the job you are being interviewed for. You are expected to bring forth your personality more than your experience through your interactions in the past. Behavioral questions help the interviewer analyze how you think and navigate yourself through conflicting and challenging situations, how you deal with failures and disappointments, whether you have demonstrated leadership or team spirit, and what are your values and objectives that drive you through it all.

Hypothetical Questions: Through this question, the hiring managers gain an idea of your ability to quickly think on your feet and pose a solution to solve a problem. These questions also include a case scenario through which you are assessed and they generally start as "How would you handle/respond to ...?"

The best way to answer the hypothetical questions is by relating them to something similar you might have faced in the past and how you contributed to resolving the issue. Show them technique through evaluating and prioritizing the information gathered before making a decision. Again, adhere to the skill set that is most apt for the job requirement. In case you have no related response for this query, let the interviewer know that you can figure it out, either by research and learning or through assistance and advice of others should you be hired.

Examine the sample questions given below:

Question #41:

Suppose you face a troubling matter with a colleague in the office. How will you handle it?

Have you dealt with any conflict in the workplace? Can you tell us about it?

Answer: Show the interviewer that you understand the hierarchical system of the professional environments and that you would report the event to the team leader. The interviewer does not expect you to respond with answers like "I will handle the situation," so refrain from giving such self-assured responses just to appear pleasant and nice in the work environment. Tell them that you had rather have the concerned authorities come up with a solution. Relate to them if you had to deal with such unpleasantness in the past and managed to handle it with the inclusion of the authorities and close it off with professional positivity.

Question #42:

How do you define your style of work?

Answer: Only make a mention of the things in your style of work that is suitable for the job you are applying for and avoid the clichéd and overused term. Be sure to use effectively terms such as 'accuracy', 'precision', 'speed', etc. that best describe the qualities which contribute to outstanding results.

Question #43:

Suppose you and your boss have different approaches to work and his is clearly in error. What would you do?

Did you ever disagree with your boss regarding some issue or work? How did you handle that?

Answer: This is not a question that you would like to answer with specific details, nor can you get away with something like 'my boss was amazing and we never disagreed.' The focus of the question is not on whether you disagreed or not, because that is something that may have happened in your career. The interviewer basically wants to decipher how you handled the disagreement. Work up your response that does not provide the interviewer with a precise answer. Say that your approach depends on the situation; at times you will just like to stay quiet for better reasons rather than complain or if you have an alternative to support you, you would respectfully suggest it to your boss.

Question #44:

As a team member, did you come across a colleague that was clearly not as motivated as the others? How did you deal with this member?

Answer: With this question too, the interviewer has an objective. Here, it is to determine how you would handle a situation wherein you have to act as a part of a team. This is an open-ended question that seeks to analyze your behavior, irrespective of your previous experiences with a team or as a team player. If you have had an experience in dealing with such a member of the team, then relay that scenario to the interviewer, talking about what the issue was and how you eventually and successfully handled it.

If you have never worked as part of a team, then just say that as a team player, your first action would be to act as a mentor for that person.

Question #45:

What if one of your co-workers or manager asked you to do something that is against the company's policies?

Answer: Although you are expected to respect the organizational hierarchy concerning your work and its related issues, the interviewer does not expect you to transgress the policies of the company by being submissive to your authorities. The main purpose of asking this question is to see if you can be convinced to go against company policies. You should answer this question by saying that you will never go against company policies whether it was your supervisor or your manager telling you to do so.

Question #46:

What if you made a big mistake at work? How will you deal with it?

What's the worst mistake you've made at work and how did you handle it?

Answer: Be truthful when you respond to this question as this will tell a lot about your behavior concerning your work to the interviewer. The focus here is how you handled the mistake and hence, it is beneficial for you to say that you informed the concerned higher authorities to avoid further damages that could be caused by your mistake. The same goes for how you will react to any mistake in the future.

Question #47:

What will you do if you learned that the company you are working for was going against the law to meet its work?

Answer: You will naturally feel like you should show your sympathy to the company or give a vague reply that offers no clear answer in order to get the job. The better response to this question is by saying that quitting the job is the least you can do if the company was doing something illegal and you were aware of that.

Question #48:

Tell us about the most difficult decision that may have made in your career?

Did you ever have to make a tough decision at work?

Answer: You can respond to this straightforward question by mentioning one or two particular events where you had to make a very tough decision in your career. You will be asked about the difficulties you faced while making that decision. What difficulties you were able to overcome while making that decision will tell a lot about your personality. Try to sound confident and avoid mentioning situations where you felt uncertain and indecisive when you talk about these decisions so that the interviewer can ascertain that you are capable of making big decisions.

Question #49:

What if you were asked to fire someone?

Answer: The principal objective of the hiring personnel is to know on what grounds you think a person should be fired. You are not likely to do what you deem as unethical and unprofessional in a work environment if it compels you to fire someone, and as such you would avoid putting yourself in a similar situation. Keep your focus and reasons to fire a person solely professional and with respect to the objectives of the company.

Question #50:

How will you deal with an angry customer?

Answer: You are very likely to be asked this question if you are seeking employment in an organization for customer service. Show your professionalism and knowledge in handling irate customers, what techniques you would apply, or have successfully implemented in the past, how you would sympathize with the customers, etc.

Industry/Company Related Questions

The primary aim of asking you questions related to their company, organization or job offer is to determine if you have done your research and you are indeed interested in this vacancy. The interviewer may even ask questions regarding your availability and flexibility with the working hours or location.

Question #51:

What do you know about our organization?

What is your impression of us as an organization?

Answer: The interviewer wants to make sure you've done your research about the post that is being offered and also their organization. They expect you to fully understand their goals and objectives as an organization and have a realistic idea of what you can give to them and gain from them concerning your job. The interviewer is not looking for any compliments but your impression of their organization and how you expect to fit in and fulfill your role to your best. Here, your focus will be on what you know about the organization rather and how you gathered this information.

Question #52:

Can you tell us anything about our products/services?

Have you ever used our products/services?

Answer: Your impression of the company's products or services will relate to the interviewer what you really know about them as well as what you feel about them. Only when you have thoroughly researched them will you have any opinion – complimentary or critical – regarding their services and products, for example, how to better improve them or how to boost their sale. Depending upon the line of work, you must be aware of the degree to which you can evaluate the company's product or services.

Question #53:

Can you give your opinion regarding our organization's greatest strengths, weaknesses, opportunities and threats?

Do you think we have a more considerable advantage over our competitors?

Answer: This complex question can only be answered if you have done a thorough research and prepared well for the interview. The interviewer is serious about testing your knowledge regarding their organization as well as that of the market. Breakdown this question as it is asked and address each case individually: the strengths and weaknesses of the organization, the opportunities that it presents and the threats that it faces. Process the concepts before providing a reasonable and concise answer for each. You can focus more on the positive concepts.

Question #54:

Have you gathered any information about the vacancy?

Can you tell us why you have applied for this job role?

What did you find appealing about this job offer?

Answer: Through this question, the interviewer wants to make sure that you understand the role for which you are applying. If you don't get a reasonable understanding of the role you are expected to fulfill through the job description, then you shouldn't even be at the interview. Make sure you convey to the interviewer that you appreciate and understand what the role involves and you are more than ready to meet the challenge.

Question #55:

Why did you choose this line of work?

How did you come into this line of work?

What appeals to you more about this line of work?

Answer: The interviewer means to indirectly ask you if your chosen line of work is indeed the right choice for you and whether you are fully satisfied with it. You are expected to elaborate your statement with an explanation as to why it is the right choice. Naturally, the interviewer will be applying this knowledge gained from you to how it suits with the job and its requirements. Show your enthusiasm and convince the interviewer how this line of work is the right one for you and how you are best suited for this job with examples from your experience.

Question #56:

How do you expect to become a valuable part of our company?

Answer: In an interview, you must show to the hiring manager that you are not here just for the salary but you fully intend to give it all you have got, not just for your growth but for the company's as well – that you are willing to contribute to the company's good reputation and make it valuable in the market.

Question #57:

Can you tell us why you have chosen this particular field and career?

Answer: This question might be asked of graduates or people without a prior experience in a particular job and are interviewing for the first time. The interviewer needs to confirm that you are in this field because you are passionate about making a career in it and not because you don't see any other choices.

Question #58:

What do you know about our CEO?

Answer: This is one of the questions that tests your

knowledge about the company and confirms to the interviewer that you have done your research before the interview. If you are applying for the job, then you must be well aware of this answer.

Question #59:

What can you tell us about our competitors?

Answer: This question is a test of your knowledge of the company and the industry that it caters to as well as the main players in it. You will need prior research in the field and a comparison of the company's similarities and dissimilarities with others in the same field.

Question #60:

Have you considered relocation/traveling (that is a part of this role)? Are you okay with it?

Answer: This is not a trick question but a general assessment of whether you are ready to travel and relocate as the company requirements. Decide these things before you go for the interview; if the job description mentions that it requires the candidates willing to relocate, then you must be ready.

Question #61:

Can you work on holidays?

Answer: You will have to say a yes to this question if you work for sales or any related customer service as these jobs require you to work on holidays to keep up with the customer demands.

Question #62:

Can you work a flexible schedule?

Answer: If you are interviewing for a job where the work shift keeps changing or rotating, you will have to show your availability as per their requirements. Be prepared for such questions if you are aware of the nature of your job. However, if there are certain days or times when you can't be available, state that as clearly as possible.

Stress Questions

Interviewers sometimes tend to make use of stress questions to determine generally how applicants react to uncomfortable and stressful circumstances. They may even be used to analyze your sense of humor. Stress questions tend to be surprising, direct and involve a psychological assessment of the interviewee through aggressive or silly questioning.

The nature of these questions may directly challenge an opinion that you may have stated, or they may seem to express negativity concerning you or something you stated. Other times, they may be downright dumb to you. The only way to deal with this type of question is to understand that the interviewer is trying to elicit some kind of reaction from you. Your greatest challenge will be not to feel offended and become defensive in your claims. Instead, be patient and try to maintain your composure as you offer your response. Do not get confused or re-evaluate your answer if you get an impression that you may have answered it wrong. It is more important to focus on how you go about presenting your answer. Don't let the interviewer emotionally intimidate you.

Go through the sample questions given below to get an idea of what you could be asked:

Question #63:

What are your reasons for quitting your last job?

Why do you want to leave your current job?

Answer: This is one question you will have to answer if you are a professional who has quit a job before.

The best response to this is, to be honest and positive. Tell them you are looking for a new better opportunity and avoid making any negative statements about your previous employer.

Question #64:

I see you have been hopping/quitting jobs. Why?

Answer: Come up with a reasonable response to this question if you have been quitting jobs throughout your career, rather than laying blame on your employers. Your answer must convince them that you won't be feeling the need to hop your job this time again.

Question #65:

How much salary do you expect from this job?

Answer: Have a clear idea of what the company has posted regarding the job offer and its pay. Research the worth of the profession and the position, and frame your response accordingly as the least amount of salary you expect from them. Stating that you will work for any amount shows your lack of preparation and puts you in a weak light.

Question #66:

Do you have a strategy to overcome your weaknesses?

Answer: If you have previously mentioned a weakness that affects your professionalism in any way, it would be better to tell them how you constantly work towards overcoming it. If you are aware of your weakness, then you must be aware of the means to overcome them and actively employing them for your benefit.

Question #67:

Are there times when you don't feel like working?

Answer: This question tests your level of honesty in the interview. Truthfully state how you feel, but make sure you mention what motivates you or how you keep motivating yourself.

Question #68:

Can we put you through a lie detector test?

Answer: It might not really be their intention to put every candidate who applies for the job through a lie detector test, but they only seek to unhinge you and check your honesty.

Question #69:

Are you physically fit?

Do you have a fitness plan?

Answer: The interviewer seeks to analyze how keenly you stick to your schedule by inquiring about your interest in your personal fitness. If you have a tendency to work out for your benefit, it is highly likely that you will adhere to the schedules too. The interviewer will relate your habits for maintaining yourself with your seriousness about the things in life.

Question #70:

Have you worked under a boss that turned out to be your least favorite? If yes, do you think you can work towards building a better relation with them now?

Answer: This is a test of your professional and mature thinking. Say yes, you would love to improve your relation with your boss. You could also say that this particular boss was your least favorite, but it does not mean you did not have a good relationship with him/her.

Question #71:

How often are you criticized and for what?

Answer: If you have already stated your weakness, then it is likely that you are/were criticized for it. You can say that you have improved with time, or you are working towards improving yourself.

Question #72:

Why do you expect us to pay you as much?

Answer: This is the direct question through which the interviewer seeks to test your confidence. You can talk about the skills you have acquired through experience and knowledge of the industry. Convince the interviewer that your position is indeed worth the salary but do state that your services will be worth even more than that.

Question #73:

Can you tell us about the most satisfying work experience?

Answer: The answer to this question will inform the interviewer about your true expectations and motivations for doing a job as the things that made you satisfied would be considered the things that you want the most.

Question #74:

How will your ex-employer think about you?

Answer: Mention the strengths you think are more noticeable about you and your work.

Question #75:

What animal do you think you are?

Answer: These questions are employed for the psychological assessment of the candidate. When you state a name of the animal, you must define why you believe it relates more to your personality.

Question #76:

Do you have a preference for a particular kind of work environment?

Answer: If you are applying for a job, then there must be only one kind of environment that you prefer – the kind that relates to the job you are applying for. This information can be gathered from the posted ad for the job. Of course, you must be able to provide a reasonable answer with your choice.

Question #77:

Do you feel any difficulty with a certain kind of colleague?

Answer: Don't start listing off the type of people you don't like to work with in response to this question. The interviewer does not care for your list but the level of professionalism you exhibit with the response. Tell them you respect diversity and you are open to dealing with people in your work environment.

Question #78:

Did you experience a great disappointment in your career?

Answer: Again, these type of questions indirectly refer to the unstated "how did you handle it" part. If you make a mention of a disappointing moment, don't delve into details that could bore the interviewer, keep this section of the information brief but focus more on how you handled it as this shows your resilience and optimism.

Question #79:

Do you have any difficulty making certain types of decisions?

Answer: This is an open-ended question that expects you to be fully honest; there's no right or wrong response to it as it may only give the employer a better idea of what you can and cannot do, should he/she hire you.

Question #80:

Has any suggestion of yours benefited your previous employers?

Answer: If you have made suggestions to your company or team that were efficiently employed and yielded productive results, then do mention them. The key here is talking about the beneficial suggestions only, not the ones you either kept to yourself or the ones that were rejected.

Question #81:

Do you tend to achieve your goals by ignoring company rules?

Answer: In an interview, never mention any instance where you did not follow or comply with the rules of the company, especially to meet your goals. In fact, you are expected to discourage such behavior.

Question #82:

Tell us about your ex-employers. Whose supervision did you admire or dislike? Why?

Answer: You can talk about the employer that was best to you and why you admired him/her. But take care not to mention any employer as the worst or specifically detail what you disliked about them.

Question #83:

Did you learn anything from your mistakes?

Answer: Take this question in relation to your strengths and professional maturity rather than feeling offended. Tell them how you have evolved and what motivated you to improve yourself.

Question #84:

What can make you angry in a workplace?

Answer: In any interview, avoid mentioning any sorts of lists, especially if they tend to put you in a negative light. Reply that you tend to act professionally on your job but if there are some issues, then you would like to be provided with some methods of taking the complaint to the authorities.

Question #85:

Why were you fired?

Answer: If you are asked this question, then be honest and let them know how you've grown in experience and professionalism and how you approach your job and as a result.

Question #86:

What is your take on punctuality?

Answer: The answer to this question should be very clear in your head. You can back up your answer and make it sound more powerful. There's no better way to stress on this point than arriving at the interview on time.

Question #87:

Do you consider yourself as a leader or a follower?

Answer: You can respond to this by clearly saying that you can integrate yourself into any role that is required of you, whether it is as a part of the team or as a leader.

Question #88:

What are your hobbies?

Answer: Mention the hobbies that are most related to your job or that prove some beneficial personal trait of yours: punctuality, goal-oriented, fitness, socializing, etc.

Question #89:

What is your favorite website?

Answer: The interviewers seek to analyze how you see or primarily use the Internet to your benefit. Give a solid reason as to why you prefer the website.

Question #90:

Was there something you disliked about your last job?

Answer: The best way you can answer this question is by stating the things that you seek to achieve in the company you are interviewing for. Here, you can prove to the interviewer what appeals you about their company: their objectives, work environment, etc.

Question #91:

If you could turn back the time, would you change something? Why?

Answer: These questions are used to test your psychology. This question in specific is used as an indicator of your thoughts about your life and career. There is no proper answer to this question but for you to maintain your confidence and composure.

Question #92:

How do you define success?

Answer: This is technically a very difficult question because different people have different perceptions of success. However, when interviewing for a job, it is best that you define success professionally. Make sure your definition is not limited to yourself only and that there is some mentioning of how you want other people to benefit from your success.

Question #93:

Besides money, what else motivates you to do your job?

Answer: A blunt and upfront response about money being your only motivator is a bad idea. Prepare well in advance for this question, understand what is additionally important to you and your career, and mention them without any hesitation.

Question #94:

Do you think you will find any hurdles in doing this job efficiently?

Answer: This question can have many answers, so be as truthful as you can while answering this question and support it with a reason.

Question #95:

What is your opinion about performance-based incentives? Are they any good?

Answer: You will have to say yes to this question but couple it up with reasons as to why you think performance based incentives are good. Support it with your past experience if you made any performance and received incentives for it

Question #96:

Do you like to be directed to a task or you prefer to find it out yourself?

Answer: This question is asked to assess your personal interest and aggressiveness while doing your job. Some people are only able to perform certain tasks when they are given directions whereas others would believe in self-direction. If you are going for a managerial job with high responsibility, you must have self-directing skills.

Question #97:

What things would you change about yourself?

Answer: Lay stress on your prime weaknesses. If you have already stated them, then try not to add more to the count.

Question #98:

What if you are rejected?

Answer: There are many different ways to answer this question but the best response is the one given with positivity and confidence. Say that you will stay in touch with the company and expect to be called if a similar position is made available in future. Don't respond that you won't be looking for any other jobs in the meantime as you have your hopes pinned on this one.

Question #99:

Do you carry your personal stress to the workplace?

Answer: Don't ever respond positively to this question: show that you are professional and mature, and you don't believe in mixing your two lives together.

Question #100:

Are you opposed to taking any drug tests?

Answer: Say that you don't mind the drug tests and would follow the rules laid down by the organization for the welfare of the company and employees.

Question #101:

How do you define an ideal leader?

Answer: The best way to answer this one is to think about the qualities of particular leader that you admire and state them one by one.

Question #102:

Why should I hire an outsider like you when I could fill this position with someone in our company who is more familiar with our work culture and products?

Answer: Confidently respond that as an outsider, you bring in a different view to the company's products or services and could contribute to implementing innovative ideas. If the interviewer specifically mentions having to deal with problems with outsiders, then question them regarding those problems and state how you hope to tackle them. Asking them why they posted the ad in the first place is not an ideal response and reaction.

Question #103:

I'm sorry, but I did not understand your answer. Could you please clarify that again?

Answer: Interviewers sometimes employ techniques to offer you additional stress. If your interviewer repeats this more than once, it is likely that he is implying this technique. Remain patient and answer as cordially as you would do.

Question #104:

Do you enjoy working under stress?

Answer: Respond to this inquiry with honesty. Clearly state if you do enjoy it or you can handle the stress, supported by your work experience. Else, tell them that you would rather have a proper plan to reduce the stress.

Question #105:

How would you evaluate me as an interviewer?

Answer: If you experience any negative feeling for the interviewer, you may want to refrain from stating it bluntly. This is an instance where you have to let go of your honesty. In fact, the interviewer does not expect you to rate him on a scale of one to ten, but whatever response you give will cause him to rate you. The motive behind this question is to evaluate your diplomacy and verbal skills. Tell them that interviewing others is not your best skill as you have not had much experience with it and you realize that the interviewer must do this in order to determine whether you are an eligible candidate.

Do the best you can during the interview and remember to present the best of yourself. Sometimes, you will need to follow the defined standards and at others, you will have to exhibit your uniqueness. The employer will carefully evaluate you and compare you with your competition, so listen carefully and craft your responses in a way that convinces the employer to note your worth and be compelled to hire you.

CHAPTER 7

SALARY NEGOTIATION STRATEGY

How to Negotiate A Best Salary Offer for Yourself

Always research and know the salary range for the position that you are interviewing for before the job interview. If you are working with a recruiter, ask him or her the salary range. You will want to make sure that the position you are interviewing for meet your salary requirements.

Job hunting can be stressful, irrespective of the fact that you may be looking for the first time or seeking out a new opportunity. The anxiety and fear can be overwhelming, especially if the needs of your situation seem to press down upon you. Add in a number of rejections and you can be tempted to take the first job that comes your way.

However, you must keep in your mind that the right moment to negotiate the salary is after you've had an impressive interview and you've been informally offered the job, but before you sign the official job offer. Many candidates do not even bring up the subject of salary negotiation because of fear or dislike of haggling. If your résumé and interview were impressive enough to land you the job, then there is no harm in openly asking for what you deserve. The hiring manager and the company have finished interviewing the candidates, and the job role is solely in your hands. Don't plainly agree to all that is offered without even trying to negotiate, because all your future raises will be based on your initial salary.

So, make use of this opportunity and ask for more money. Given below are prep tips to ensure you have a successful salary negotiation with your next job offer:

Know Your Personal Worth and Value

Preparation done well in advance always serves well later. The only way you'll get paid just for what you deserve is by knowing the pay rates for your position in your industry and area. State your value in the market to the interviewer – not what salary you desire – as it validates your request. When you go for negotiating your salary, have an exact number with you.

Talk to People

From working professionals in your industry, who you may or may not know, to other recruiters, hiring managers and even organizations, inquire the range of salary for your field based on the job title, years of experience, education level, and location and how it can vary. Further, you can gain insight from them as to how you can increase your value. Note that you must not contact the employer who has hired you as this shows your ignorance of the matter.

Select one number

Your research is likely to yield you a range that represents your market value. You may try to appear humble and ask for something in between the range. Don't undervalue yourself because your employer will try to convince you for the bottom half of that range. Thus, it is important for you to negotiate with a precise number in the top of the range, so even if the employer negotiates with you – which, he certainly will try to – you may still end up with a salary that you deserve and are satisfied with. Being specific with your salary number shows the employer that you have done your research and looked into your value in the market.

Consider other options

Decide on the salary offer that is too low for you to accept. Base it on your financial needs and market value. Be willing to walk away if it is too low. Walking away from an offer is never easy, but if you are considered good enough for one company, you can be the best for someone else too. On the other hand, if the offer is considerable but the employer refuses to increase the salary, then try to negotiate for other things, such as a signing bonus at the date of hire, stock options, , more vacation time, professional development course and tuition reimbursement, year-end bonus, flexible and telecommuting work schedule, etc.

NEGOTIATION STRATEGIES AND TIPS DURING THE INTERVIEW

Walk in With Confidence

Walk in with confidence and bring a positive vibe with you. Keep up with that attitude through the interaction and you are sure to walk away with an offer that makes you happy.

Prove yourself

Before starting the conversation about the salary, ask questions to understand more about the company's needs, preferences, and priorities. In response to that, provide them with vague solutions of what you can do and craftily ask for the salary by putting forth the number of your market value. If you are asked about your current salary, then give them the correct number, along with the additional benefits that you may be getting, and move the conversation to what you're hoping to achieve with this change of job, through your acquired experience and skills, how you have added to your market value and how you expect to continue growing. Do not lie about your current salary only because you feel you are underpaid.

Avoid ranges and ask for more

Even though your research will get you a narrowed down range, do not make use of the salary range when negotiating as this displays a weakness in negotiating and that you are willing to concede to what the employer will put forth. Instead, give an exact number and don't shy from asking for more. Be the first to give the number and this number that you present first will provide the flow for the rest of the conversation. If it's too low, you will very likely be ending up with a final offer that is lower than what you expected. Asking for more allows the employer to negotiate too, in turn making them feel like they are getting a better deal.

Do not get desperate, anxious or pushy

Stay positive and kind but firm, and don't let your anxiety surface. Maintain your composure no matter how anxious you feel and avoid emphatically stressing your points. You don't want to appear desperate and pushy.

Be clear about your needs

Lay out a prioritized list of your needs as part of the salary negotiation to make the employer understand your interests. Don't give away too much information and avoid listing any personal needs (like the need to pay the rent, cover your loans, etc.) Make a mention of your experiences and achievements to aid you in stressing your value.

Listen to the employer

Listen carefully to your employer and pay attention to what they are saying. By understanding their priorities and limitations, you two can work towards finding a mutually benefiting solution. And don't be afraid of rejection or give in at the slightest hint of it; the idea behind the negotiation is that both parties must align with each other's interests, and it will very likely begin with a no. So, think quickly and counter with a response that expresses your point.

These are the 7 Strategies you must follow when it comes to negotiating salaries;

What has the company got to offer you?

Be prepared for the negotiations: gather as much information as you can about the company. While it is important to identify the role of the company in the industry, what it stands for and what it does, as well as the responsibilities of the job and the scope for promotion in order to set a possible salary range, it is also necessary to investigate more about the company's finances, its turnover and for how long it has been in the business.

Gain insight into the company's stability in the market, its ability to perform and deliver, and as such pay timely wages to the employees along with other benefits.

What do you have to offer to the Company?

Identify your worth, your market value in order to have a strong hand in the negotiation process. Without knowing what you are worth in the market, or having any idea about what your position could offer, you will be making a sorry case for yourself and hence feel powerless to get it going your way. You have already been given the offer informally, and they know they want you to fill in this role. So, don't undervalue yourself by not having proper preparation, understand what you are capable of and how you can contribute to the company. Ask for the salary that well compensates for your work.

What is the competition paying for this job position?

Get an idea of what is being offered for this similar role from various sources. Make note of not just the salary but consider all the additional benefits that come with it. Find out what the competition to the company has to offer and set an estimated pay range to guide you in the negotiations.

How much do you want to make?

Additionally, make a critical assessment of what you want and prioritize it. Analyze how much you are making against how much you want to make. This will help you further understand how much you need to have to cover all your basic needs, what range of salary you would like to make to cover your financial needs, what range of salary you can compromise on that fits within the range of your market value and finally, what range of salary is the deal breaker that will cause you to turn away from the offer.

What are the additional benefits being offered?

Don't discredit the other benefits being offered with the salary. It could be that the company offers you a minimum salary, but they have additional benefits that interest you and as such make your work more interesting and satisfactory. Find out the additional non-salary related benefits the company has got to offer to its employees and ask for them instead.

Are you prepared for the salary negotiation?

Your education combined with your work experience and skills should give you an edge to expect a higher salary. Add in your willingness and preparation and you will be successful in coming to a conclusion that benefits both you and the employer. Don't shy, cringe or feel hesitant at the idea of negotiating; employers tend to value an employee that is self-aware and dedicated to work, and as such offer them the salary they deserve.

When should you walk away?

If the company is unwilling to negotiate with you, or is unable to compensate a better salary or benefits for your work, as understood by you to be the salary range that you cannot agree to, then it is better to walk away from the offer, Don't enter a negotiation with a minimum salary in your mind, and give up as soon as the negotiation progresses. If a company is not willing to negotiate, then it is probably not a company that you would want to work for. The company's unwillingness to compromise or negotiate is an indicator of issues within its work environment: either they lack respect for their employees or they are unable to maintain stability in the market or offer growth that as an employee you would be seeking. So, it's important for you to know when to walk away and be prepared to do so.

Employ these strategies to successfully negotiate for the salary you deserve. And more importantly: Do negotiate for the best salary offer!

CHAPTER 8

CLOSING THE INTERVIEW-
7 WAYS TO ASK FOR THE JOB
AT THE INTERVIEW

At the end of an interview, many job hunters are curious to know about their performance. They want to know if they did very well, and if there are possible considerations for the prospective job. But most of them are perturbed as they do not know the reply they might get after asking for the job. You would not want to ruin an excellent interview by blowing it up with a wrong question, after all the efforts you have put in the interview. This gets you thinking: "how do I go about asking for the job when the interview is about to wrap up?" Most people tell you that you need to request for the job, but not many of them even know how to go about it, not to talk of telling you how to.

Many job hunters make use of a passive approach. With this technique, what they do is decide not to ask for the job. Very often, this method is interpreted wrongly by the hiring managers, as they feel that the candidate does not have an interest in the job. However, the approach works infrequently. As a job hunter, you are expected to be curious about the job if you really have a burning desire to work for the company. In most cases, this desire to work for the company is even what most employers look out for in their prospective employees during an interview. And when it is realized that the passion for the work is lagging, most of them tend to agree in their subconscious mind that you don't have much interest in the job anyway. This is a very dangerous assumption which could end your dream of future employment at the company.

In some occasions, many hiring managers love to hear you ask for the job. To them, this shows your eagerness and enthusiasm and it's flattering. It is true that it can be a difficult question to ask. We are often afraid the answer will be "No." Some of us may also feel that it is impolite or too pushy to ask such a direct question. Some of us may just be shy.

As said earlier, in most cases, the usual conclusions from hiring managers are that if an interviewee fails to ask for the job, he/she is just uninterested. Yet, many candidates don't see it this way, they feel asking for the job isn't right, and this could make them be rejected once and for all– basically, this is rampant among candidates who have been on the job hunt for a very long time now and are beginning to get frustrated already. It's not easy being rejected each and every time you do an interview. You really can't decipher what went wrong in your last interview and why you didn't get the job. This makes some of the long time job hunters uncomfortable about asking for the job, with the thought that maybe that was what blew up their previous attempts to secure a job. Others term asking for the job as being too forward or desperate.

The fact, of course, is that you don't want to be tagged someone you are not. You don't want to be thought of as proud, obnoxious or pushy. What you really want to do is make the conversation a friendly one with the interviewer. In this case, you wish to find a common ground to know when to ask the question and which tone you should use in asking. The better you get to know about your interviewer, the more comfortable you feel in finding the right words to use in asking for the job. As a job candidate be confident and *ask for the job*. You have everything to gain by showing the hiring manager your desire for the job opportunity.

. There is no big deal about asking for the job anyway, isn't that the reason for the interview in the first place?

Some approaches work well in most cases while some don't work often. We will be distinguishing these approaches so as to know which of them is the best. The response of the interviewer is vital as this will help you in realizing whether you are fit to get the job or not.

To get started, here are seven strategies you can employ on the theme of "how to ask for the job?" They mean almost the same thing. Read through them and see which of them sounds a little bit like you. Try to get used to it, memorize if possible, and use it conveniently at the end of your next job interview.

1. **Straightforward Strategy**: "I want to work for your company– I have lots of passion and enthusiasm for this position."

While the most rampant strategy, this method is embedded with its own problems. This strategy works great in sales, but not in a lot of other fields. In sales it shows that the job candidate is a closer. The reason is because it is mainly based around the need of the interviewee and not the interviewer's point of view. A candidate should not use this approach without having a good "gut feeling" on the overall success of the job interview.. Also, it depends on the temperament of the interviewer; so, it is advised that if at all you want to use this strategy, you should have read the kind of person that your interviewer is, and ensure he is not the type who takes offenses over every little thing. I always encourage and coach job candidates to *ask for the job*. Ask for the job with confidence. "I am very excited about working for your company. Will you give me the opportunity". After you ask for the job, remain silent and let the interviewer respond. The interviewer might say, "we are interviewing other job candidates and we will make a hiring decision within two weeks". The most important strategy in 'asking for the job' is showing the interviewer your desire for the job opportunity.

2. **Feedback Strategy**: "So, how did I do?"

With this approach, all you are trying to do is place the interviewer in a position that he/she may not be able to escape telling you how the interview really went. What I will just advise is that if you are not ready to face the reality of how you did, don't ask this question. Do not go seeking for the answer when you cannot handle the truth. If you feel you did not do well, it's better you ask questions on—how he/she thinks you can do better next time, rather than asking for feedback on your entire performance. Well, if the interviewer is the type who does not talk too much—his response goes a long way in determining if you did well or not; depending on the tone of delivering his feedback. "We are still considering many candidates for the job, which of course you are a part of, we will inform you about the actions taken in the next few days."—with this answer, you should know that your fate stands in the pool of the candidates. If you did better than most of the candidates, you could have gotten a straight answer like—"you did very well, wait till we inform you about the proceedings in the next few days."

3. **Next Step Strategy**: "I'm really enthusiastic about this job and working with your team, what's your next step? When will you be making a decision? Do you still have questions you want me to answer?"

As much as this strategy is one of the favorites among the sales people, it also has its disadvantages. This approach utilizes a technique of basic assumption which is mostly rampant in the sales world. Depending on how you performed during the interview, you are also likely to have answers almost the same as that of the feedback approach. Be sure to get strong replies like—"wait for the next few days when we would have finished making decisions, we will call to tell you about the next steps." On the other hand, you may also hear something like— "You know there are many candidates for the job, and we are really going to take our time to make the decision, if there's going to be a next step, we will let you know in the next few days; we will get back to you when we are done, you don't need to get back to us."

4. **Objections Strategy**: "Do you still have doubts about how well I could handle this job? If yes, what else can I do to convince you that I'm the right person for this job?"

This strategy can also work effectively and even perfectly well when the position being interviewed about has to do with a sales rep. It's a big risk asking this sort of question in a position that does not relate with sales representative.

It works well for a sales position simply because it goes a long way to show your closing skills. For a normal position that does not include a sales position, you may have risked gambling by not asking the right question you should have asked. Even if the interviewer has made decisions that you are the best fit for the position and then he still goes ahead answering you in a "No" tone, you might still be bewildered as you may not be able to decipher how genuine the response is. The interviewer has already decided that you are the best man for the job; his decision stands solid no matter his response, as decisions have been made.

5. **Ranking Strategy**: "I feel my background and skills are just perfect for this position, and I am very interested to know how I rank in comparison to other candidates for this position."

To some extent, this tells the interviewer how self-confident you are, and it also goes a long way in displaying the fact that you have a competing spirit, which may just be one of those top qualities that the company wants from an employee. This is a classic strategy that can help you make your discovery as to whether you will truly get the job. It's an insight to the chances of getting hired by the company. Through this approach, you stand a chance of getting some excellent feedback because it's the question you asked. This is an advantage because it's a morale boost for you if you get a great feedback at this point. The hiring manager is opened to telling you how well you have done; in relation to how well you have already thought you did. If the response you get does not decode the fact that you are likely to be considered for the job because you seem to be one of the favorite candidates for this particular position, don't waste your time expecting any call from them, just find another fit elsewhere, because probability of this one happening is almost zero.

6. **Fitting-in Strategy**: "How do you see me fitting in with your company?"

Asking this type of question only means that you are ready to hear the truth from the horse's mouth. If you do not see yourself as a good fit for the job, and you likewise do not like to get your morale level down, do not use this approach. Truth is bitter, and you may find yourself losing hope when you could still be the winner.

This can be effective especially when a major criterion is how sensitive you are to others. If the response you get is not great and mind blowing, if casual word like the "fine" or something similar is being made use of, or if the interviewer tells you they have to make their decisions through all the candidate's performance, and see how you fit into to the company, then it is noteworthy that you are not a part of the high-ranking candidates. Someone who is one of the highly ranked choices would never get such casual word for an answer as the interviewer would be excited beyond that. Again, don't waste your time unnecessarily waiting for a phone call, move on swiftly to the next.

7. **Scaling Strategy**: "If you are to put me on a scale 1 to 10, how do you think I would do in the position?"

For most circumstances, this approach is one of the best for positions other than sales rep. This approach goes a long way to imply that you are indeed after the truth about your performance, and you really want to be corrected appropriately. Your quest for getting a feedback is well managed in this condition

This is not a strange approach to the interviewers, and this in return raises your chances of being told how you really did by being honest enough for you to deal with. To get more genuine response, you can also ask a question like "If I were to make that a 10, what more could I do?" This approach truly opens you to your stance concerning the job in hand, and it's also the best chance you have at deciphering anything else in the mind of the interviewer – it may also be an opportunity to erase any doubts or wrong impression the interviewer had of you earlier.

Just as you have read from these seven strategies, they have their advantages and disadvantages. Each of these strategies has when to or not to use them; it's now left to you to read how well the interview has gone and be able to know which strategy is best to use. The approach you use in asking for the job matters a lot; you may not want to look desperate, or even sound bothered. In some scenarios, some questions may get someone disqualified earlier in the job hunt if it sends out a wrong signal to the interviewer. Read the interview and the interviewer; you should be able to know how well you have performed to some extent. This should help you in asking the relevant question.

For someone who has done woefully in the interview to ask the 'Ranking Strategy' question: "I feel my background and skills are just perfect for this position, and I am very interested to know how I rank In comparison to other candidates for this position?" looks somehow awkward! You know quite well that you did not impress your interviewer, so you don't have to boast about your skills. It's definitely a wrong choice of question to use as this can lead to automatic disqualification.

It may be best to use the 'Next Step Strategy' question: "I'm really enthusiastic about this job and working with your team, what's your next step? "When will you be making a decision?" this sounds truthful as well as enthusiastic.

CHAPTER 9

10 QUESTIONS YOU SHOULD NEVER ASK IN A JOB INTERVIEW

Your interviewer may give you a chance to ask any question you may have towards the close of an interview. This opportunity is golden, as it gives you a chance to sound intelligent, prepared, and enthusiastic about the position. This is indeed a great opportunity to impress the hiring manager or interviewer with the homework you have done and your knowledge of the position and the company. Asking questions that you did not prepare to ask beforehand, on the other hand, could completely revoke your chance of getting hired for the job. Whether you are currently on a job hunt or not, try as much as possible to widen the scope of your knowledge. You need to know whether you have the rights of asking your interviewer's a particular question or not.

The aim is not just to ask questions for asking sake; the objective is to ask intelligent questions— reasonable ones that depict you have been attentive and that you have not been lazy when it comes to doing the necessary research works basically on the position and the company as a whole. At the very least, you want to ask something. Based on research, it is evident that most employers agree that one of the wrong questions they have heard their candidates ask is "no question'. This is even the most infuriating reply for any recruiter because it does not only depict that you may not be interested in the job, it may also denote that you are clueless about the job, and you do not even know what to ask at all. This merely depicts you lack passion towards the job, because if you are curious and enthusiastic about the job, you are supposed to have questions on your mind no matter how awkward they may seem. With this, you are only trying to send out signals to the hiring manager that you are not a truthful type of person, and this could terminate your possible consideration.

Questions that should not be asked in an Interview:

1. Avoid questions related to benefits

What's the salary? You are not supposed to be asking

about salary (and salary negotiations) and company benefits if you haven't sold yourself(knowledge, skills, abilities, value to the company) to the interviewer or been offered a contract. These are not expected to be discussed until you have been extended an offer. Likewise, this same technique applies to a period of illness and vacation days. Some questions make it look as if you have assumed you have been offered a contract; it is best to avoid these questions so as not to sound derogatory or pushy—unless, of course, your interviewer is the first to mention it. The fact remains that you are not yet an employee of the company, asking them such questions make them feel uncomfortable with you- they may assume you are more concerned about the benefits than the job, or you need medical help. The company may not wish to employ someone like that. Be smart!

2. "Can you tell me something about the company/ job?"

This visibly depicts that you have failed to do your homework. How did you manage to get to the interview table without knowing about the company? This goes a long way and tells about your lack of interest in the company, and if you are not keen on knowing where you want to work, it shows you have less enthusiasm for the prospective job. Employers may regard you as unserious and instantly decide that you will no longer be considered for the job even if you might have had a great interview. So, asking about the company or anything that was already answered in the job description is risky. You are the one that is meant to be asked such question, not the interviewer.

It is advised first to go through the job description. Do not continue asking questions about management, when it is explicitly stated in the job description that it will be an individual customer's service role.

3. "Are there any internal job opportunities?"

This particular question is silly in the sense that you look unserious about the real business you came to transact. It's obvious that you already have an idea of the position you are being interviewed for, but you don't have much zeal towards that post— this is one of the many reasons that can make someone ask questions about internal job opportunities. You are applying for the job you are being interviewed for, not the jobs that are likely to open up in the near future, so you don't have to expend time talking about future opportunities when you have not even secured the current job. This can totally backfire and make you look foolish in the end. Don't try it!

4. "How often do reviews occur?"

Why are you so concerned about getting reviews? This question is a bit absurd in the sense that it makes you look suspicious. The interviewer might be as well concerned that you are scared of getting negative reviews, and this has a lot to tell about your prospective behavior in the company when you get hired. No one who is of a good behavior should care about reviews that much. Well behaved people do not need reviews to get praised, everyone sees their good deeds easily, and it does not necessarily have to go down to when reviews are been issued before they get a regular "thumb up" from their bosses for being so diligent. Be careful of this question; do not make them see you as what you are not, going in the wrong direction.

5. "May I arrive early or leave late as long as my work is completed?"

There are part-time jobs, and there are full-time jobs. Do not ask this question in a job interview. These are answers you could have found out before an interview. Asking if you can arrive late for a job that even your presence is required earlier than the reporting time your employer gives you is absurd. There are jobs that customers start rushing in as early as 6 a.m. Why ask if you can make it to work by 8 a.m. then? This clearly shows that you are overly concerned about your personal needs than the company's desire. And the owner of the company may not want someone who will put less input in his work. Workers are always expected to perform far beyond the expectation of their bosses, the moment you start asking questions about coming late, it shows that you are not ready for the job, and when this happens— no one is ever going to consider you for such job.

6. "Can I work from home?"

A lot of companies give employees the option or flexibility to work at home. You will find out " in time" during the interview process whether you will have the option to work at home. Sell the interviewer on your knowledge , skills and abilities and what value you will bring to the company *first*. At this period, your top priority is selling yourself to the company. Furthermore, asking this type of question to early during the interview process shifts the focus on your needs. So, it is better to be calm and observant when you are there for a job interview and the interviewer might answer this question without you having to ask it. Save this question toward the end of your interview when you have time to ask questions.

7. Can I show you my references?

Asking this question may look too desperate or pushy. It's obvious you are in the haste of using your references as a lifeline. Don't be surprised if the company care more about your knowledge and skill than they do care about your references. Like the game of dating, same goes for interviewing. "It's important to showcase your value to your date so that he/she would already be looking forward to the next date with you." To be too quick to offer your references, talk about it only when questions are asked about it. Your reference is a lifeline for you, don't use it before you get to need it.

8. How soon do you promote employees?

Okay, this is an important question, but it does not really have anything do with the content of the job which the job interview is all about. Apparently, this question may make the hiring manager wonder if they can maintain you in the company. If a candidate asks this question, he might be regarded as someone who is proud. Employers want employees they can manage, even though it's a matter of the company getting to buy what you have to sell to them, but the fact remains that the company will be paying your bills, they may just feel they deserve some level of respect as the question may seem quite obnoxious at such stage of the interview. As soon as you are discussing the job offer, you can go all the way and ask about the rate of salary increments and all that, but not when the interview is still ongoing.

9. Am I entitled to a personal office?

A tough question to ask, it is. You may not know if you were never told, but the question sounds odd. Of course, it is normal to wonder if you will get your personal office or not, but will getting your personal office be the decider of whether you will accept the job offer or not? What you prioritize is quite important to your prospective employer; don't be like a student— who thinks too much about his bad handwriting, rather than his bad grades. While this issue may be crucial to you, the question is probably not appropriate for the first job interview without a good explanation of why you are asking.

10. Do you monitor your employees on the social media?

The first impression about this question is that you have a skeleton in your closet or negative information online. This might insinuate that you are the type who posts any little thing about your life on the Internet. Disagreements and misunderstandings may occur at a workplace; the last thing that employers want to find out is that the issue has already gotten to the Internet. This is quite derogatory, and it shows you have no significant interest of the company at heart. Learn to keep some personal things to yourself, especially your recent broken relationship. Often, females go about depressed, and ranting about their recent breakups with their boyfriend on the social media, this may go about creating a wrong impression of you to your prospective employers. Don't think your recent rough/vulgar post wouldn't be seen by anybody from your workplace even if you are not friends with anyone of them on such social media, these posts have a way of circulating, trust me.

The bottom line is that you should have an idea of the company. Ensure you have done your research very well, both on the Internet and from the current staffs of the company, if possible. Don't ask 'selfish' questions, most especially if you do not have an offer yet. Don't ask questions that might create a bad impression of you. For successful job interviews, stick more to the questions about the job, primarily based preparations, and the discussions during the interview. Always note that when an interviewer asks if there are questions towards the close of a job interview, it is your opportunity to— gather information about this position you are looking to secure, and the employer that is important to you, and also, show to the interviewer that you have done some research about them— this indicates that you are actually passionate about the job, and you are not just wasting your time.

CHAPTER 10

DRESS CODES FOR INTERVIEWS- IMAGE IS EVERYTHING!

It has always been said that "The first impression lasts longer." The first impression you make on a hiring manager is the most important one. The way you look and what you put on would be the first thing that your interviewer will notice about you. Apparently, he begins to form his judgment from here, which in return is likely to affect his final conclusion about you. This is the reason while in most cases, it is still important to dress professionally for a job interview, regardless of the work environment.

What's the appropriate dress code for an interview? You'll, of course, want that first impression of you to be a great one. Bad impression may go a long way in affecting your overall performance in the long run. In general, the impression that an interviewee dressed in a navy blue suit and tie is going to make a much better than the candidate dressed in shabby chinos-pant and a t-shirt.

Dress code differs organizations by organizations. The way bank workers dress varies from the way engineers do. Still, there is usually little or no difference on how to be dressed for an interview. But when one is confused on how to dress for an upcoming interview, it's best to make inquiries.

I will be making some suggestions on what you can wear, and what you should not wear; for professional, casual and start-up companies when you want to make the best impression.

HOW TO DRESS FOR A PROFESSIONAL INTERVIEW

Men

- ❖ Neat haircut
- ❖ No jewelry
- ❖ Suit (solid color - navy or dark grey)
- ❖ Long sleeve shirt (white or coordinated with the suit)
- ❖ Belt

- ❖ Tie

- ❖ Dark socks, conservative leather shoes

- ❖ Limit the aftershave

- ❖ Trimmed nails

- ❖ Portfolio or briefcase

TIPS FOR MEN

- As much as you would apply professionalism in your speech and actions during an interview, it should not just end there. Men are usually advised to dress appropriately, formally and in a professional way for an interview. When we talk about dressing formally, it means wearing a suit.

- It does not make sense dressing shabbily for an interview no matter what the dress code of the company for the job may be. As said earlier, if you are confused about what to wear, try as much as possible to do your research, and if you can't do research; just ensure you do it in a conservative manner.

- It's important that you wear a suit to interviews. A "suit" entails a jacket that matches (preferably a dark-colored blazer), pant, a long shirt (solid but light color preferably), a tie, coordinating, socks and dress shoes.

- Choose to wear a suit you are comfortable in. This is what raises your confidence level. Being at ease is paramount. Dress in a comfortable way, look and act your best by dressing smart. Don't wear an oversized blazer, let everything fit you. When I say fit, I do not mean tight! Don't go and wear the suit you wore during your 17th birthday because you want to look smart. You won't be comfortable, and that's when your confidence level begins to drop. Be smart!

- If the suits don't fit perfectly right, get a new one! It's better to invest in a new one than to go for an interview looking like an idiot.

- Don't go rough for an interview. It goes a long way to tell your interviewer that you're not organized. Let your dress sense be just accurate. Let your clothing be thoroughly clean and smoothly pressed. If you don't know how to press a cloth smoothly, find someone to do this for you, better still; get a dry cleaner.

- It's not a normal day that you just jump out of bed and put anything on. It's an interview; you want to speak and be heard. Make sure you have fresh smelling breath for the interview. If you're a regular smoker, try as much as possible to avoid smoking before the interview.

- Another important thing about your dress code is your hairstyle-- you should understand that it's an interview and the interviewers do not have the deep idea of who you are. Don't go for an interview with a haircut that is to trendy. Practice modesty in every aspect of your dressing. You do not want the color of your suit to get all of the attention during the interview.

- After the first interview is the second interview. Many candidates make the mistake of dressing casually for a second interview. This shouldn't be the case because you're not yet employed. "You have not even been offered the job yet, and you have already started dressing any kind of way, what about when you get the job, would you be able to follow the company's directive?" That's the way some employers see it, and then decide not to consider such candidate for the employment no matter how well he/she performed in the interview.

- The way you dress is definitely the way you will be addressed. Dress very unprofessional and you will be treated with less respect. Dress like a professional person and you get the respect of the bosses!

- Your dressing isn't complete without a good shoe. Ensure you choose the shoe that matches the color of your jacket-- preferably a black shoe for a black blazer, and a brown shoe also goes with a brown suit. Make sure your shoe is well polished and shiny. If you don't have a good shoe, invest in a new shoe, you will need it for the job anyway. I hope you also know that the color of your belt must correlate with the color of your shoe. This is very important, don't wear a black belt on a brown shoe, you will go in there looking like you are not polished professionally.

- If you are the hairy type, try as much as possible to shave your beards and mustache at least 2 days before the day of the interview. You need to look neat and clean for your interviewer.

These things have a way of affecting your confidence, especially when you get to the premises of the interview and you realize how rough and dirty you are compared to other candidates. This is where your level of confidence begins to drop.

Always remember that you are going for an interview. It's not a normal day that anything you wear goes. So, following these laid down guidelines shouldn't be a big deal for you if you are really serious about getting the job. There's nothing professional about being dirty, stinking, and rough. Dressing in an unprofessional manner for a professional job interview makes you look like the least likely job candidate to get hired. Moreover, you are not dressing like this every day. It's not every day that life gets so serious as a job interview, is it?

Women

- ❖ Tailored fitting-suit
- ❖ A comfortable suit skirt (must cover the knee)
- ❖ Simple blouse

- ❖ Simple and professional hairstyle

- ❖ Neatly done nails

- ❖ Use Light make-up

- ❖ Avoid high-heeled shoes

- ❖ Don't use any bracelet, if possible

- ❖ Avoid dangling earrings

- ❖ Be very conservative if you wear jewelry

- ❖ Pantyhose should be neutral

- ❖ Briefcase

TIPS FOR WOMEN

- Just like men, women are also expected to dress modestly for a job interview. It's not a social event; it's a job interview. Don't go for a job interview dressing anyway just because you feel you are a female and not many things matters. No, many things matter!

- Basically, a woman is expected to wear a shirt with a skirt or pants. But when you are not sure about what to wear, try and find out from close sources. And if you still can't decipher what to put on, ensure that you are as modest as possible.

- Wear what will make you be at ease and peace with yourself. Being comfortable in what you wear goes a long way in improving your level of confidence. Wear a smart and fitting suit; don't go for an oversize or an undersized. Wearing something too tight may make you look horrible, and before you know what's happening, a male interviewer is more into what you wear, rather than what you are saying.

- Also, if the suit is an oversize, you can always find a tailor to help you slim it down before you put it on for that interview. Smartness is everything, dress smartly!

- Don't waste your time thinking about the color of suit you should wear. Like I said earlier, it's not a party. Just decide on using a navy suit straight away. It's not a fashion parade show, so you don't have to waste any time deciding this. Simplicity is a sign of modesty. Don't go for suits with designs, just something simple.

- Don't go for the flashy colors; let the 'top' you are wearing for the interview be cool in tone. Cool colors are conservative enough. Avoid colors like yellow and red. These colors shift unnecessary attention to you and make you feel as though something is wrong with you the moment everyone is looking at you. Yet, truly, nothing is wrong with you other than your yellow blouse.

- Avoid the use of heavy make-up, let it be at the back of your mind that you need to be conservative and its a job interview. Professionalism should be your watchword, when it comes to wearing make-up. Just use a light make-up if need be. Use your best judgment on the make-up that will give you the *best look* for the job interview.

- Have well manicured nails for the interview.. If you need to fix your nails, make sure you have short nails, and don't go for the flashy colors . Use colors that are not noticeable, if possible, use a neutral color.

- Avoid the use of heavy jewelry Lower the use of jewelry-- why put two rings on your fingers? You shouldn't even use any if you can do without it.

Also, accessories used on hair should be kept to the minimum.

- Women have so many types of shoes they wear on outings (club, date, parties, etc.) Don't mistake an interview for a social event; avoid the use of shoes that you wear on those occasions. Avoid the use of high-heeled shoes, most especially; those with thin heels. Its advisable to wear some comfortable low-heeled pumps or flats in black or a color that matches your outfit.

- You know perfectly well that you won't be comfortable in it, so don't try using it. Aside the difficulty women face in wearing these shoes; the shoes are pointed and this makes them to produce sounds while walking on a hard surface. Wearing this to an interview can be so embarrassing, especially when you enter the boardroom and everyone starts looking at your leg. It's advisable to use a moderately low-heeled shoe; which is in a perfect, non-scuffing, condition.

- Let your dress give you a very professional and polished look that exudes confidence. You are at the interview to- Get Hired!

- Wear a conservative hairstyle that will make you look very professional and polished. Do your homework and research the company culture and see how other employees wear their hair. You want the interviewer to focus on your knowledge, talents and skills not how trendy your hair looks or how creative your hairstylist is.

Let it always be at the back of your mind that you are going for an interview. It's not a normal day that anything you wear goes. So, following these laid down guidelines shouldn't be a big deal for you if you are serious about getting the job.

A 'dress for success image' shows respect for the interviewer, the company and yourself.

Your image is everything , so be your best professional and polished self in every job interview.

CHAPTER 11

TELEPHONE INTERVIEW TIPS AND STRATEGIES

Nowadays, companies use phone interviews as a platform to pre-qualify candidates' interest and expertise after going through their resume. This kind of interview also gives a candidate an opportunity to decide whether a job is worth doing the follow-up to or not.

Here are some guidelines and strategies to ensure your next phone interview is a success:

1. Find a quiet location.

The first key to a successful phone interview is finding a quiet environment. Do ensure you are in an environment where you can hear clearly on the phone, basically, an area with a good cell phone reception. Ideally, make use of a landline, where it's quiet and calm enough to give the interview your full attention. Phone interviews are a bit hard because the only tool of communication you employ is your voice. This is a disadvantage to many people, especially those you hardly hear what they normally say in person. The interviewer's impression of you is shaped by all the sounds coming through the phone. A soft voice might sound nervous, especially when there are noises coming from the background again. The interviewer first contacts you, make sure you can talk on the phone for at least 15 minutes.

If you're unable to isolate yourself when the employer's representative makes his or her initial call, ask to schedule a specific time for the phone interview. This ensures you will do the interview when you are fully prepared and in a quiet environment where you can speak without interruptions. Schedule the phone interview just as you would do any face to face interview. Also, isolate yourself from distractions and background noises. Don't have your interview when you're surrounded by lots of noise and loud sound . If the call is on your cell phone, make sure that you are audible enough to be heard by the interviewer. Also, ensure that your battery is fully charged.

2. Do your research.

Take time to have a deep knowledge of the company. If the company has a website, find time to read through, you will definitely have a big picture of the company before the interview, rather than going for the interview to ask simple and obvious questions. Recently, you might have sent your resume to more than one companies; you may get a call from one of these companies without your prior notification. Having done your homework by doing research on these prospective companies, you will not have difficulties in identifying which of these firms you are being interviewed from and what the company is about. You have just flopped the moment you are asked by an interviewer what you know about the company, but you are unable to say anything reasonable about what the company stands for. So, if you are the type who send applications to 10 companies weekly, ensure you do enough research about each and every one of them because you wouldn't know which of them might be calling you soon. Companies do have competitors too, it would do you some good finding out those who are in the same industry with the company, it will help you during your discussion as it shows you do not only have the in-depth knowledge of the company, but also knowledgeable about what's going on in the market.

3. **Have your already prepared responses handy.**

Very often, most phone interviewers follow an identical mode of questioning. They do this with the sole aim of screening you out or placing applicants on the short list of best candidates. One interesting thing that makes a phone interview easy is that you have the time and space yourself, and no one is monitoring your body language and movements. Due to this, it's better if you can prepare a clean sheet of paper. Ensure you find somewhere to note the possible questions, and answers, or any other information you would like to talk about. Here is a list of questions most phone interviewers ask. Write down your responses and practice them by saying them out loud to yourself.

• Introduce yourself?

• How did you learn about this job?

 • How much do you know about this company?

• What are you doing currently?

• What is your monthly income?

• Why are you looking for a new position?

• What are your strengths?

• What are you weaknesses?

• How would you react in the face of challenges?

• What are your worst and best traits?

• What's your biggest dream for the next five years?

• Would you like to ask any questions?

Let the interviewers know you are very smart and professional with these questions. Having prepared answers to them and mastering what to say very well, it goes a long way in helping the way you build rapport with them. At the end of the day, it would not seem like a question and answer type of chat, it would be just like a discussion that it is meant to be.

Ensure that you do not cram your responses anyway. There's a difference between mastering something and cramming it. Don't go into an interview hitting your hand on your head just because you have forgotten what you crammed; that's pretty silly. Moreover, questions different from these are likely to be asked, the responses are to help you flow, it's like you read the mind of the interviewer and found out all the questions he/she would ask.

4. **Add your interviewer on professional websites.**

Adding or following your interviewer on a professional website like LinkedIn is a good move. It reveals some information about who they are. Check their educational background and their past job experience. Through this, you can find out if you have any interest in common. You can never tell; it may be your best chance of getting connected to them. Most of these people do not mind if you did your research to such extent, don't go around thinking it's a big deal connecting with such people on such platform, and that they may not find it pleasant. In most cases, they are only appreciative of the fact that you found time to learn about them. There's nothing obnoxious about connecting with your prospective employer on LinkedIn, if they weren't in such shoes, you could connect with them anyway: so what makes it any odd? Moreover, it's not like you found them on a dating site.

5. **Dress the part.**

This is less of the physical appearance. Mannerism goes a long way in deciding your fate during a phone interview. You don't want to sound arrogant when that's not who you are. How people see us isn't just in the clothes we put on, it also shows in the way we act. Your manner of speech also depicts to a large extent about who you are, since the only thing the interviewer will be using in forming the conclusion of you is your 'voice' and response to questions. It's only a phone interview, and you are expected to dress appropriately, it sounds odd, isn't it? But to be frank, this stuff is psychological. The way you are dressed may affect the way you talk on the phone.

6. Keep your documents handy.

Have your necessary documents, especially your resume, next to you. Phone interview gives a great advantage as you can quickly flip through your document in case you are asked any question and you cannot easily remember.

7. Don't get too serious, smile.

Your interviewer will notice everything about your voice since that's the only thing she can hear. She will definitely pick up on your tones. She will reckon with it so much because she's not in contact with your look and unique set of eyeballs. She needs to have the positive impressions of you, so let her hear you grin big. So go ahead, and release the muscles on your face. Smile all the way and make a good impression of your calm and uneasily daunted personality.

8. Let the conversation flow.

This simply means that you should not take everything too serious. Let the conversation flow. Free your minds that it is an interview, though never forget what's at stake. But believe me; your employer wants to employ someone with a good sense of humor, too. Someone he or she can easily have a good conversation with discussing work life balance. It's not always about the next client. Be personable and professional during the telephone interview.

9. Speak audibly.

Speak audibly enough for your interviewer to hear you. If you have a problem with your phone, quickly notify her to the reschedule of the interview date. If something is wrong with your voice, let your interviewer know. It's better to reschedule the interview than to get fired before you even get started. Take a bold step by letting her know you have a sore throat, cough or catarrh affecting your voice. Be wise!

10. **Show enthusiasm!!**

Let it show in your speech that you have utmost passion for the job. Also, demonstrate it in the sound of your voice. Like, Fantastic! Don't be so nervous to the extent that you will not ask detailed questions about the position. The questions you ask will reveal the motive behind the questions and the way you go about asking goes a long way to show how enthusiastic you are about the position.

11. **Don't be too forward!**

Being too forward in a phone interview won't help matters. Don't spoil your high level of esteem and confidence with a "being too forward" attitude. This goes a long way in affecting your employer's choice, as to keep in touch with you or let go. Save the salary and benefits questions for the latter discussions. However, do not hesitate to hit the nail on the head if your interviewer asks you questions relating to how much you think the job offer is worth.

12. **Show you are ready to answer more questions**.

Ensure you also ask if she has questions for you once she has finished providing answers to your questions. This depicts a lot about how self-confident you are, and your level of readiness in securing the job. Not many interviewees have such level of confidence to ask this question, so, please ask. The worst that can happen is that you don't have any answer to give to the question you are asked, still, this does not diminish your effort in any form.

13. **Move forward!**

As the interview comes to a close, do ensure to ask about what the next step concerning the job is, and when you are expected to get a follow-up notification (SMS, mail, call) from them. It shows that you have the interest of the job at heart.

14. **Show a sense of appreciation!**

After the call, do ensure that you send a brief note of appreciation to your interviewer. Don't write an epistle, you wouldn't want to sound too desperate, or make it look as if you are begging for the job. Always have it in mind that this is a buyer and seller scenario. You have what the company needs to progress, so why beg to be hired? In a brief note or email sell the interviewer on the value that you will bring to the company and you look forward to the next step in the job interview process.

15. **It's not a normal phone call.**

Phone interviews should never be attended to the same way you attend to a phone call from your best friend or mom. It is not only when it's a face-to-face interview that you should get serious. Many candidates are always eliminated through phone calls, and you may not want to be a part of them. You can't have a phone interview with music playing in the background; neither can you tell your interviewer to give you a sec while you check what you're cooking in the kitchen! This may be your best chance of hammering it. Take it seriously!

Be clear and concise with your smart interview questions and answers during your telephone job interview and sell your knowledge , skills and abilities to get that face to face interview.

CHAPTER 12

7 INTERVIEW SKILLS THAT WILL GET YOU HIRED

Communication skills top the list of the seven most important skills an interviewee needs to have in order to secure the job. Hiring managers are constantly looking at client job descriptions that state that candidates must have "excellent communication skills." Most of them have gotten so used to seeing it that they frequently forget to mention this as a requirement when describing a position and this is a mistake because it is the most important skill a candidate should possess. This implies that you need to be articulate enough to be able to pass good information while discussing. You don't just speak because something has to come out of your mouth, or write because you just need to use your pen; when you talk and write, you ensure that you are passing on information, and not delivering a dry piece of speech or article. Hence, excellent communication skills do not only refer to one's proficiency in how to speak only but also implies a good ability to write articulately and express yourself for readers to understand the information you are trying to pass across. Basically, it entails the capacity to express your thoughts articulately and professionally.

Effective communication skills also include the potential to listen. The fact remains that listening is hard. In fact, listening is more difficult when you are nervous. You are surrounded by panels of interviewers who keep throwing questions at you intermittently. It may even be hard to breathe, talk less of listening. So, you really have to be confident enough to listen to each and every word being spoken. Moreover, listening has a long way to do with how efficiently one can flow in a discussion because if you listen more intently, then you should be rest assured you would have more reasonable questions to ask, other than asking questions that don't relate to what has been discussed in any manner; it's a costly interview mistake.

2. The Willingness to Learn

The willingness to learn is a critical attribute everyone has to have. Lifelong learning goes a long way to show how ready someone is to be a leader—the saying that learners are leaders isn't meant to smooth talk anybody who lives to learn every day because that's just the fact. Hiring managers also have it in their mind that people who are committed to the learning process, even outside their field, knows how to critically think outside the box. These are the kind of people that companies want. Not just people who knows nothing other than the theoretical and practical aspects of what they were thought in school as an undergraduate, but people that will tell you why they want to learn computer coding , even though she is currently learning fashion designing— which does not, in any way, correlate with the accounting she studied in school. Commitment to lifelong learning and development should inspire you— let's face it, this will go a long way in inspiring your prospective employers, as this shows you would not have problem learning the new things the company may have to impose on you.

Your employers are interested in the things you have learned recently. They also have so much interest in what you are currently learning, and the things you have in mind to learn in the near future. They know really well that someone who is into continuous learning will bring so many innovations and ideas into the organization as these types of people have the capability to think outside the box and add tremendous valve.

This should never be mistaken for the skills you have in your resume alone. You should make your interviewer realize you have vast knowledge, and your brain capacity is wide enough to learn new things about the company through your recent and current learning. Let them know you take lessons in Chinese language every weekend. Don't lie about this if you are not learning anything yet, try to be on the safer side, you don't know when you might be needed to chat with a Chinese client. Just list a few things you have in mind to learn soon, and tell them how you want to go ahead in achieving them.

3. Customer Service

Customer service is indeed one of the skills one needs to have in order to make it in a corporate organization. There's no business enterprise that does not deal with customer's need. Customers are the people with the need, the buyers of what you sell. If you do not serve them well by providing exceptional customer service , you may find it hard to grow your business. This is why customer service is one of the major skills that employers are constantly on the look out for. Believe it or not, nobody would like to employ someone who does not know how to relate with customers. That's why someone with good customer service and human relationship skills is always a plus, not someone who frowns when attending to clients like he/she is being forced to be present at work.

It should be understood that this is indeed one of the most significant differences for the person who is going to make it in industry.

Identifying who customers are and being able to attend to their needs satisfactorily is one of the essential characteristics needed from you. "What have you ever done to support the success of a customer before?" You may be asked this kind of questions in order to decipher what you understand about this essential attribute.

4. Teamwork

It is noteworthy that an enterprise cannot be successfully run if the individuals that make up the team do not act as a team. Just like in a game of team sports, all of the players need to play together to win; so does it also implies to an organization. Employees have to come together, bring their ideas, brainstorm on how to carry out the plan before they go ahead achieving the goal. This is why teamwork is one of the vital skills that hiring managers look out for during an interview. Most corporate employers believe that the major difference between academia and industry is the culture of teamwork that pervades the industry.

As a student, you do most of the activities alone—assignments, tests, exams, projects. The only time you do team work is when you are divided into groups, and you have to come together to discuss the given topic so that you will not end up getting a bad grade in the course. However, this is not the case in corporate organizations. Most of the work done are teamwork based, and you constantly have to come together as a team to achieve success in the long run. If the company fails, you fail.

"Have you ever motivated a team to success before?" "What are the attributes you need to have to be a good team player?" "What is your opinion about working together as a team?" "How often do you form a team when you need to solve a critical problem?" These are questions you should be prepared to answer in a job interview. Many hiring managers make a 'team player' attribute as an essential determination guiding their decision to hire an employee.

5. Initiative

How often do you initiate a fresh strategy to refresh or improve something? Do you have the ability to initiate something that will benefit the company? How often do you take steps first before others decide to follow? These are primary questions that go a long way in answering how you take the initiative in bringing up new ideas.

Many companies will investigate this attribute through reference checking. Let your references know that you have an upcoming interview. Remember to tell them about your great achievements; don't be so certain they remember most of the things about you. Your reference is a lifeline here, ensure you use it wisely.

6. Ability to Adapt

Constant change is one of the usual occurrences found in every industry. Employers want to find out how you have behaved in some cases of sudden change in your environment or circumstances surrounding you. Employers may want to know how you will react when the company transfers you to another department. This, in essence, will help them to reveal how adaptable you are to changes, and how responsive you are to stimulus.

These questions may be asked at an interview in order to decipher your level of adaptability. "Why do you think a business have the need for a change?" "Tell me about your experience in maintaining or exceeding your usual performance in the face of some unexpected, dramatic change?"

7. Growth

Your desire for growth is one of the major skills that will secure you a job. Employers are not just looking for some mediocre job candidate who never makes an effort in growing daily. They are not seeking to employ someone who will stay in the same spot for years, just doing the job being told to do without going extra miles developing ideas and tactics that will help the company grow. Do you demonstrate the overall behaviors, skills, knowledge and desire to grow? How driven are you about improving yourself? --Hiring managers and employers look out for this trait all the time.

Always demand the best of yourself.

Conclusively, every company has a set of winning characteristics it considers when making the decision to hire. These seven skills described above represent what industry employers in this global marketplace are looking for. Ensure you study them and make sure that you are ready to demonstrate examples of these qualities in yourself throughout the interviewing process.

CHAPTER 13

HOW TO SUCCESSFULLY ASK FOR THE JOB

As discussed earlier in 'chapter 8,' there are seven major approaches an interviewee can use in asking for the job, but the difficult task is deliberating on which of these strategies will earn you the job.

Don't ever be afraid to *ask for the job* in a job interview.

The best way to end an interview is to show that you are interested in offering your skills, experience, time and energy in exchange for employment in a way that demonstrates your eagerness. Do this by closing the interview with questions such as, "I am very confident that my solid work experience , skills and performance will exceed your expectation in this position and that we would work well together. Have I given you all the information you need to offer me the job?" or, I"m very interested in this job; is there anything preventing you from offering it to me right now?" A direct , honest approach to illustrating you are enthusiastic is the best way to avoid appearing desperate. Demonstrate a calm and confident demeanor when asking for the job.

However, the only thing that is constant is 'change'. Asking for the job in the *appropriate manner* can be the deciding factor in landing your next job. The mannerism of which you ask the question may just be an eye opener to the interviewer- about how optimistic and confident you are towards working with the organization. It's only better to go for the job straight. If you have done well during the interview, you would be employed anyways. On the other hand, if you did not perform up to expectation, it's not likely you get employed. So, why not boost your little chances of getting the job? Whether you think you did well or didn't do well in your job interview always ask for the job. Never underestimate yourself or the overall success of the job interview.

Think of asking for the job as a "game-changer" in the job interview process to get hired.

Some approaches are just a "No" for the interviewer. Some questions are just too direct and aggressive that it makes the interviewer not to be at ease with the interviewee. Very often, the interviewer has a lot going on her mind due to the plight she finds herself in choosing who is best for the job. Going ahead to ask a question like "When can I start working on this job?" may seem somehow too desperate for him, considering the fact that there are still other great candidates for the job. But whether this tactic would work out or not depends on how subtle and polite you were while asking, and also, the temperament of the interviewer. So, as I have reiterated earlier, it's best to read the interviewer and find out which approach will work for him best. Different strokes for different folks, it is.

"So, when do I start?" A question like that is about as aggressive as you can get at the close of the interview. It may knock the interviewer for a loop and appear to be overly aggressive, but some people think of it as closing the sale. For some people, it has worked. For others, this approach may not feel comfortable, or have the same effect. Your comfort level with the close-- whether you are aggressive, passive and polite or somewhere in between -- will depend on your personality, the interview situation and the job for which you are applying.

Note that: **Different strategies work for different candidates; it all depends on your personality.** The moment you understand the kind of person you are, it would be easier to go with the strategy that will work for you without unnecessarily acting what you are not. This is the case of "being oneself." The remaining part now goes to the other candidate(s) you are competing with, and what the employer is on the look out for.

Mr. George, the manager of a Fortune 500 Company, held a final interview with two high ranked candidates from the previous interviews. He was on the verge of choosing which of the two candidates is best suited for the job.

At the first interview, Mr. George was amazed by the question asked by the interviewee when she said: "Well, I'm sold! When would you like me to start?" Beth, has just graduated from a university about a year ago and had has several job interviews which hasn't resulted in employment. Beth implemented a job interview strategy that increased her confidence, successfully sell her knowledge, skills and abilities that leaves a lasting impression with hiring managers. Mr. George was very impressed with Beth's confidence and the value that she was able to communicate as a potential new hire. Beth asked for the job at the close of the job interview.

Mr. George told her that there is still another individual whose fate has also not been decided, and that he has to interview with him first before he would be able to know which of them is best for the job. Beth smiled and furthered by asking him when she's expected to hear from him. He told her that she would hear back from him in the next couple of days when the decisions would have been made. They exchanged pleasantries as Beth found her way out of the office. Beth is going to email or send a handwritten note to Mr. George that will summarize her enthusiasm and desire for the job and state the "value" that she will bring to company in three strong benefits-driven statements. Mr. George was really impressed with Beth as a job candidate and what has left a lasting impression is her confidence, great attitude , asking smart questions,value-added statements and asking for the job.

The second candidate, Michael, also had high-level achievements and skills which almost correlate with that of Beth. However, her style of asking questions was quite different— he seemed more passionate about the job as he made lots of inquires about the position and ask relevant questions that have to do with the company's future. This in return goes a long way to show his level of concern and enthusiasm towards the company's success. He also furthered by stating the reasons he feels he's the best candidate for the job, by boasting about his skills and achievements, and the things he can bring into the company that will increase their output. Mr. George also told him he has not made his decisions because there's still another candidate up for consideration and he might need to ruminate very well about one or two things before he would be able to come out with which of them is best fitted for the job.

These are two wonderful candidates for this business consulting position, aren't they? Mr. George will have to consider who is best for the job by taking into cognizant the position to be occupied. These are two great candidates with two different personalities. Beth is more persuasive and forward. It is evident that she has a strong negotiating and penetrating power which is ideal for a business consulting position. Michael, on the other hand, is less persuasive, but more inquisitive and seem to be more subdued; this makes him a good job candidate as well. Michael wasn't able to successfully sell his skills, knowledge and abilities to Mr. George in a very clear, concise and compelling way. He didn't ask for the job and only sent out a "generic" follow-up thank you letter to Mr. George. Mr. George called Beth and offered her the business consulting position. Asking for the job during the job interview and the value added thank you follow-up letter was the "game-changer".

What I would advise is that you should do thorough research on the position you are being interviewed for if not clearly stated in the job description, so as to know which approach to employ in asking for the job, successfully.

In every step of the job interview process always sell your **knowledge** , **skills** , **abilities** and **the value you will bring to the company.**

- Without changing your personality strategize on how to bring an interview to an end, you should have some of these few points in the back of your mind:

  Look the interviewer in the eye and say, "I want this job, and I will be a profitable hire for your company." Then, be silent and let the interviewer respond. You want to show the interviewer that you are 'proactive' and 'want this job opportunity.'

- One of the most important things is the right picture of you. Ensure you leave your interviewers with four skills you would like to be remembered about after the close of the interview. It's also best to ask them if they need to know some additional information about you— it shows that you are ready to tell them as much as possible how much of great qualities you have embedded in you.

- Your interest in the job matters a lot to your prospective employer. If you need the job, why show an attitude like you are the only one with the achievement? So many people have more than what you think you have. Let them know the additional value you can provide to the company, be curious about the job.

Asking for the next step in the job securing process is not a crime, in fact, most employers appreciate this. It never makes anybody mad when you ask for next stage in the process. It's important for you to know the next step so that you can be informed when decisions would have been made, and not sitting back waiting for a call that is never going to happen when you should have moved on. Ask for their contacts if need be.

- While closing an interview, it's good to be professional about it. When you are done answering questions thrown at you by the interviewer, it's best to use an honest approach when the interview is about to come to an end; take into consideration asking some of these questions:

- Based on my background and the skills and experience we discussed, how well do I fit the profile of the candidate which you're looking for?" This question is blunt enough as it will help you know what the manager thinks of your performance.

Given what we've just discussed during this interview, do you have any concerns about my fit for this position?" this question differs from the first one in the sense that you are trying to know what skills and experience you need to have before you can get the job. It tells the interviewer that you are willing to learn and ready to take corrections. This puts you under possible consideration for the job.

- Furthermore, ensure you state your interest in the job as the interview comes to an end; you can make use of these approaches to be described:

- Based on my research and what we've discussed, I would like to work for you in this job. How soon will you be making a decision?" with this sort of question, you have just been successful in making the interviewer realize that you are ready to work for the company. Your interest in the job matters a lot if you want to function well. This is what most employers are concerned about, and you have just made them realize that you have the interest of the job at heart and you are certainly ready for the company.

This discussion has made me even more excited about this job opportunity, and I would love to be the person you hire. Is there anything else you need from me before you make a decision?" This clearly shows that you are one hundred percent ready to work. It's more like asking about the next stage; in which case, you might just be told what next to do.

Depending on the present situation, choose a question that mostly applies. Don't stop there, go ahead and appreciate the interviewer his or her time.

Ask for the job and get hired!

CHAPTER 14

HOW TO SUCCESSFULLY FOLLOW-UP AFTER AN INTERVIEW

You have perfected your resume, linked up with recruiters, and had a great interview. But if the next thing you do is wait to hear back from the company, you might as well say a 'goodbye' to the position.

It is critical in the job interview process to send out a follow-up thank you letter or note expressing your interest in the position and the value that you will bring to the company. Never send out a "generic" follow-up thank you letter or note. In the email or letter always continue to sell your knowledge, skills , abilities and value that you will bring as an employee. This is the winning formula for a thank you letter that will leave a lasting impression with hiring managers.

It's up to you to take the leading role when it comes to landing your dream job — even after the interview is over.

"It's not adequate to send out online job applications and go to interviews when seeking employment— you need to go the 'extra mile' every single time you try.

"Many job hunters think that an interview is over the moment they depart the premises of the interview location, but in the real sense, the recruitment process continues." Companies go over resumes and interview notes to help them make a decision — and a good follow-up can tip the scales in your favor."

So, as soon as you have completed your job interview , put down the relevant things, from what transpired (and what didn't), to what is critical to you about the role. This information will help you compose a good and effective piece as a thank-you note.

The following morning, send a short email (not an epistle) or handwritten note to your interviewer to let them know you appreciate their time, you are greatly honored to have been considered for the interview, and you are still very well interested in the position. Let the appreciation come first, and then mention a specific moment from the interview. Whatever it is, by briefly talking about it, it goes a long way to emphasize that you were attentive, and you are truly interested in the company. It's also a good way to remind them of a high point from your interview.

"Say something along the lines of: I'm really excited about the opportunity you are offering; this seems like an exciting time for the business, and the role is a great fit for my skill set and experience. If you need any additional documents or information from me, do let me know.'" He says these two sentences show how enthusiastic you are and reinforce what a perfect fit you are for the job.

But don't think it's time to relax after sending this email. If the hiring manager gave you a time frame for the process, ensure you follow up more when you should have passed into the next stage of interviews. If it happens that you don't have an exact timeline, aim for a second follow-up 10 to 16 days after the interview, if you still haven't heard back.

TIPS TO A SUCCESSFUL INTERVIEW FOLLOW-UP LETTER

There are many weapons to use in landing for your dream job. You need to have your weapons completed in your arsenal before you can win this course, and that's just the basic fact. A follow-up letter is more like a shield used in protecting oneself in the battlefield; as though one may hold the sharpest of swords, but if the protecting shield is missing, then the soldier is as good as dead.

- The point is just that you really need to follow up your job hunting game with a letter as soon as you have completed the job interview. The letter should mainly contain 'appreciation' and then, the other major reason is to 'fill your lapses' or whatever way you did not perform up to their expectations during the interview.

- **Write the follow-up letter immediately after the interview**: write the follow-up letter the moment you get home. If you don't have the chance to do it that same day, as a result of getting home late, or you were too tired to think, ensure that the following day does not elapse before you mail the letter to them. Don't hesitate to do this real quick, as your hiring manager may term your lateness as lack of interest, especially when loads of other candidates have already sent their follow-up letter.

- **Address the best moment of the interview**: As said earlier, try as much as possible to make a brief reference to one of the best moments of the interview. This will not only make them remember who you are, but it also goes a long way in making them realize how much you were so deep into the interview, and how high your level of commitment in serving the organization is. This also makes you stand out amongst all the other candidates as many of them may not know this trick.

- **Address every interviewer**: Give the interviewers something to talk about by addressing them individually. Write each letter for each person. The fact remains that not all of them has the same great opinions about you; some are not impressed, while some are greatly impressed, the rest are even indifferent about your performance. This does not only go a long way in emphasizing individual point of views about you, but it also gives you a great chance of being recognized the most among all the candidates.

- **Showcase to them your knowledge about the company's culture**: One of the best ways employers decide if a candidate is best suited for the job or not is through the candidate's ability in revealing how much he knows about the company. No one will doubt your ability to fit into the company.

Be positive in your tone: be positive in your words. Don't write a letter with the tone of someone who has already lost the job. Let them be amazed of your optimism about the job. Also, make sure that there are no grammatical blunders in your letter; proofread it till you are confident it's hundred percent error-free.

The magic that follow-up letters do cannot be overemphasized. With the fact that many candidates went for the interview, but just a few wrote a letter, not to talk of sending any follow-up letter, it should be noted that through that letter, your candidacy is strengthened by being one of those few candidates who sent one. Not many people who went for the job interview leave the scene with the same level of interest they had before. Many people didn't do research on the company in the first place, so they did not really know what the job entails. These kind of people never sends a follow-up letter. Subconsciously, many hiring managers simply believe anyone who fails to send a letter after the interview is in the category of these uninterested sets of candidates.

By following the tips described above about writing the letter, you will have the capability to write a follow-up letter that is compelling enough to strike in your favor.

Writing a follow-up letter is a must, it does not only showcase your interest in the job; it also helps in developing a communication with the hiring manager after the interview is over. This developed interaction can be a stepping stone to securing the job.

However, the question to be asked is: "how is it best to do the follow-up to a job?"

As said earlier, development of communication with the hiring manager is crucial. So, it is best to consider the same way you have been conversing with the hiring manager since day-1 and continue to use that same medium.

Bottom line is that, if you stay in contact with your interviewer, you increase your chances of getting hired for the job.

Be sure to write your winning follow-up letter!

INTERVIEW COACHING BONUS

22 WAYS TO HAVE UNBREAKABLE, UNSTOPPABLE AND POWERFUL CONFIDENCE IN JOB INTERVIEWS

Going for an interview isn't one of the easiest times to have the most comfortable of smiles on one's face; it's hard to achieve. You are curious and anxious about what to come, and if you keep acting like this, it can go a long way in affecting your morale. To be successful at a job interview, confidence is the major key. Having confidence in yourself is an essential key to interview success— no matter how learned, knowledgeable and well-dressed a person is for an interview, if the confidence level is lagging behind, then there isn't much that such an interviewee can do to his/her chance of securing the job. However, the best thing to do before an interview when you are feeling nervous is to learn how to build unbreakable, unstoppable and powerful self confidence.

If you don't convey confidence in your experience and skills, why would a prospective employer want to hire you? Plenty of psychological evidence shows that acting confidently is the best way to feel more self-confident because our attitudes shift to be consistent with our behavior.

Here are 22 tips to having unbreakable, unstoppable and powerful self- confidence in job interviews:

Play a power Anthem in your head

This might sound crazy, but it really works. Every one of us has this powerful song that just makes us feel like we can conquer the world. This will make you feel like you don't worry that much about the 'interview' and ready to answer all the questions confidently. Call it your power anthem!

Think of all the People who believe in you

Over the years, some people must have said one good thing or the other about you. Let these words flow in your head, go through your endorsements again if you have to and remember your references. There are people out there who recommended you for a reason. It will make you feel better knowing that even if you didn't get the position, it doesn't mean you have a bad life.

It just means there is a place reserved for you elsewhere.

Think of yourself as an asset

Remind yourself how valuable you are. Feel like you are an asset and they need you to make the company grow and succeed. If you keep telling yourself how broke you are and how bad you need a job, you'll go in sounding desperate and hopeful. Instead, tell yourself "I can do this and that for this company and will be a great asset." It will help you focus on your strengths, which is what all employers want to hear! This is indeed a great confidence boost.

Erase all negative thoughts

The last thing you need for an interview is distractions. This is what negative thoughts will do if you allow them space in your head. Though it sounds easier said than done, but it's very necessary. Negative thoughts will take your mind away from the possible positive outcomes. To be more focused and confident, you need to have a positive mindset. Remind yourself that you are a great job candidate to be called for a job interview — many people don't get a shot at all.

Don't forget why you got called in the first place

If only you could keep in mind the number of candidates who sent their resume for the job, you would realize how valuable and respected you are to have been called for the interview. This is adequate for you to know that you truly are amazing and capable of rocking this interview!

Connect

Your utmost desire is to connect with people during your discussion. Build a database of information that your interviewers will be able to tap relevant points from, instead of trying to show off your achievements or your dazzling suit. Stop Impressing, start connecting!

Take deep breaths

Being nervous for a job interview is normal. You are going to be faced by someone who cares less about whether you have the job or not, and throws the questions at you anyway he/she deems fit. But, make sure you regulate your breathing technique; don't breathe too fast, the faster you breathe, the more nervous you get. Calm down your nerves by breathing slowly before an interview. Take a deep breath, and do it slowly and clearly—you need to have that oxygen back into your brain box so that you can think without pressure.

Speak life to yourself

Speak life to yourself! You need to be self-motivated that you can do it before you can do it. You are what you speak! Be kind to yourself by saying good things to yourself. Even when it feels as if your heart is about to come out of your mouth, keep speaking life into yourself that: "I can do it! There's no limit to the extent I can go! I am the best! I am going to excel! I will go in there and perform excellently! They cannot bring me down!"

Curb anxiety through relaxation exercises

Let your mind be at the present moment. Do not think too much about the interview. Relax yourself to curb anxiety. You can stretch your body till you begin to feel good.

Think of possibilities

You are what you think about yourself, and what you think about yourself is what forms the image of you in your head. Imagining success is enough to boost your morale and self-esteem, which will, in turn, have a positive impact on your performance. Before you enter the interview room, begin to visualize a successful interview: Imagine how you walk tall into the room, exchange pleasantries with the interviewers, and ace all the questions with confidence. Truly, your success is possible.

Prepare!

Prepare, prepare, prepare! The only way to fake confidence you don't feel is to prepare and practice strong answers for commonly asked questions. Without preparation and practice, you are likely to sound scared or rambling, neither on a route to presenting a confident demeanor to an employer. You have no pressure on you if you are totally prepared for the interview, you have weapons of words in the arsenal of your brain already, and this even makes you wonder what kind of question they may ask you that you wouldn't be able to provide a relevant answer to. Preparation is nothing, but a confidence booster!

Smile

One of the best ways to boost your confidence level is to "make friends" with your anxiety before it overwhelms your ability to reason well. So, keep that slight smile on no matter how tensed you are feeling on the inside. The more you smile, the less anxious you get.

Actions speak louder than voice

It's not always in the speech, sometimes, it's about how composed you are. So, compose yourself very well. Walk in straight, stand tall, make eyes contact and exchange pleasantries with a bold handshake.

Be professionally dressed

You don't just dress casually for an interview; it goes a long way in affecting your confidence level; especially when you get to the premises of the interview center, and you realize how gorgeously the rest of the candidates are dressed. If you don't know what to wear, make inquires before the interview. Be formally and professionally dressed! Be smart!

Be attentive

The best form of speaking is listening. Practice a good communication skill by being attentive. If you could not hear what was said, let the speaker know you didn't so that he/she can repeat the question. If you can't hear what is being said and you cannot spell it out for such person to come again, that's the moment your confidence level begins to drop. So, feel free to talk, because effective communication is vital if you want to answer the questions being asked accordingly, as well as, appropriately.

Be brief in your speech

Let your answers be as brief as possible. You don't need to talk too much before you make sense. The moment you start saying too many things at the same time, your mouth begins to get dry, and you may need water to control your speech. So far you have made sense in your brief answers, there's no need talking further except you are asked further questions about the same stuff.

Avoid the use of improper words

Avoid the use of inappropriate language. Don't use slangs/vulgar terms in a job interview. You can be shown the exit the moment you do so. It's not a comedy show, be wise!

Don't be cocky

Attitude plays a key role in your interview success. There's a big difference between being confident and being cocky, with a thin line of demarcation separating them. There is a fine balance between confidence, professionalism and modesty. Even if you're putting on a performance to demonstrate your ability, overconfidence is as bad, if not worse, as being too reserved. The moment you realize they have the wrong impression of you already, your confidence level drops. Don't allow this to happen.

Don't be desperate

You don't need to be desperate; there's no point in begging people to buy what you sell when it only makes it seem as though you are selling fake stuff and you only want to cheat them. You appear desperate and less confident once you start begging for the job. Be cool, calm and collected!

Be confident and honest

Don't tense yourself unnecessarily. The calmer you are, the better your chances of landing the job. Also, be honest. Don't try to implicate your character with a few evasive answers. Say the truth and let your integrity be affirmed.

Be humble

No matter your previous level of experience or exposure, be humble during an interview. In fact, the interviewer might be younger or less experienced than you, but that does not matter. Wear a cloak of humility and your chances of getting that job are further improved.

Make use of your power pose!

So, before your next job interview, spend 3 minutes at home before you leave or where ever you can have 3 minutes of privacy, in your I-just-scored-a-goal power pose. Hold that pose for 3 minutes. Your confidence hormones will respond to the pose, and you will actually be more confident! Feel that victory! *Embrace it!* Then, in the job interview, remember your power pose – stand up tall (or sit up straight if seated). Don't be afraid to make big gestures and take up space – reach out confidently for that handshake. Smile. Speak clearly and with sufficient volume to be heard. Be happy and confident.

CONCLUSION

Landing your dream job is a great journey; the one you have to trudge without getting weary. As tired as you could get, you just have to keep moving till you reach your destination— till you are successful.

It is not only important but necessary to attend an interview at a company before you get hired for a job. Interview is a medium used by hiring managers to decide if one is fit for the job or not. It goes a long way to show that the credentials provided are not just the only criteria for selection, but also the ability to defend your accomplishments.

When it comes down to a job interview, there is nothing of such referred to as 'over prepared', the only term we can have after all is an 'overwork'. Before that big interview, it's better to stay up for weeks learning the arts and science of how to ace the interview— doing this wouldn't only help you perform extraordinarily, it will also make you stand out from other candidates.

In order to assist job hunters in their quest of landing that big job, this book has done justice on how to be successful in job interviews. The skills, tips, and strategies discussed in this book are enough for anybody to have a successful interview. All you have to do is take your time in studying chapter by chapter, into details, the useful information embedded in this book.

The chapters in this book will go a long way in helping you to— increase your confidence even when you've been faced by past rejections, strike the perfect balance by helping you to articulate your story, tackle tough interview questions with ease, ask relevant questions, help you negotiate your best salary, know how to close your interview by asking for the job, follow up the interview in the right manner and finally standing out in a job interview in a way that would make you irresistible to hire.

Ensure you learn these job interview tips, skills and strategies you need to know to get hired. The only thing standing between you and getting hired for the job you want is having the right job interview tips, skills and strategies to have a successful job interview.

Finally, if you enjoyed this book, then I'd like to ask

you for a favor, would you be kind enough to leave a review for this book on Amazon? It'd be greatly appreciated!

Get Hired for the Job You Want.

I *believe* in **YOU**!

ABOUT THE AUTHOR

Robert Moment is an Interview Coach who specializes in job interview tips and strategies that help professionals achieve career success by maximizing their knowledge,skills and abilities to get hired for the jobs they want and get paid more in their careers.

How Can Interview Coach Robert Moment Help You

Get Hired for the Job You Want?

CONTACT INTERVIEW COACH ROBERT
MOMENT

EMAIL: Robert@HowtoInterviewTips.com

LEARN HOW TO INTERVIEW SUCCESSFULLY IN
THE NEW GLOBAL MARKETPLACE

VISIT www.HowtoInterviewTips.com

CPSIA information can be obtained
at www.ICGtesting.com
Printed in the USA
LVOW04s1532220816
501365LV00019B/796/P